Western Australia

Northern Territory

Queensland

South Australia

New South Wales

Victoria

Tasmania

DARWIN

BRISBANE

PERTH

ADELAIDE

SYDNEY

CANBERRA

MELBOURNE

HOBART

# AUSTRALIA

## A Handbook for Living and Working Down Under

**Fiachra ÓMarcaigh   Jessica Classon**

ANGUS
& ROBERTSON
PUBLISHERS

ANGUS & ROBERTSON PUBLISHERS
16 Golden Square, London W1R 4BN,
United Kingdom and
Unit 4, Eden Park, 31 Waterloo Road,
North Ryde, NSW, Australia 2113.

This edition first published in the United Kingdom
by Angus & Robertson (UK) in 1989
Irish edition first published in Ireland
by the Mercier Press in 1988
Text copyright © Fiachra Ó Marcaigh and Jessica Classon 1988, 1989
Typeset in Great Britain by Poole Typesetting (Wessex) Ltd., Bournemouth
Printed in Finland

British Library Cataloguing in Publication Data
  O Marcaigh, Fiachra
  Australia: a handbook for living & working down
  under. – Rev. ed.
  1. Australia – Visitors' guides
  I. Title II. Classon, Jessica
919.4'0463

ISBN 0 207 16381 2

For Deborah, Mark, Kate and Bob,
our friends in Australia.

# ★ Acknowledgements ★

The authors wish to thank the following for their help: Cathy Murphy, Bob Malone, G. L. Robins, Mary Woods, and the staff of the Australian Embassy, Dublin; Caoimhin Ó Marcaigh; Jane Agnew; T. J. Byrne; Karen Heatley; Mike Murphy; Lesley Osborne; Seumas Phelan; Siobhan Phillips; Sharon Quigley; Graeme South; and Mark Classon, for putting up with us.

# CONTENTS

# INTRODUCTION:
## What's All This About Australia?

You are thinking about, or have decided on, trying Australia for a while, perhaps for a lifetime. Maybe you just want to visit and see what all the fuss is about. Despite the huge interest in Australia at the moment, solid, up-to-date information is hard to come by.

You want detailed facts and advice on how to get there, land a job, find a place to live and get some idea of life in this society. There are plenty of guide-books suitable for tourists, but hard facts on the nuts and bolts of getting set up are scarce. We hope this book will fill this need, from visas to vehicles, and help you on your way.

Australia is a marvellous place, with many interesting work opportunities, but they do not come easily. The country has an unemployment problem too and there are many immigrants, as well as Australians, competing for a place in the sun. Life is harder than it has to be if you do not start off with the right attitude, skills and information. We had a great time during our year there, but a book like this would have helped.

The decision whether to go or not is up to you. This book will let you weigh up the pros and cons and put you on the way to getting the most out of the Lucky Country. As they say down under. 'Go for your life!'

# 1

# GETTING IN
## Visas

Anyone who is neither an Australian citizen nor a New Zealand passport holder must have a visa to enter Australia. Naturally, the type of visa you look for will depend on what you intend doing in Australia. As with visa applications for any country, do not presume on getting one instantly and do not quit your job, buy your ticket, or go around settling all your old scores until you are certain of success.

All enquiries and visa applications should be addressed to the Australian High Commission or Consulate for the area in which you live. They are:

- South Wales and southern England: Australian High Commission, London.
- North Wales and northern England: Australian Consulate, Manchester.
- Scotland, Northern Ireland, Northumberland, Tyne and Wear: Australian Consulate, Edinburgh.
- Full addresses and phone numbers for these offices can be found in Chapter 12.

## ★ Visitor's Visas ★

These are issued to people who are going to Australia for a short period – usually less than six months. People normally

11

covered by these visas are tourists, those visiting relatives, going on business trips or getting medical treatment.

To get a visitor's visa, you should complete the Application to Visit Australia (form M48) which is available free of charge from the High Commission or Consulate. Return the form with:

- Your passport, which must be valid for the period you intend to stay in Australia.
- A recent passport photograph, which you have signed on the back.
- If on a business trip, copies of correspondence which shows the nature of your intended visit.
- If you have previously applied for migration to Australia you may need to show proof of your intention to leave following the visit for which you are seeking a visa.

People on visitor's visas are not permitted to work, to take up a course of study or to settle down. Generally, it is impossible to change your status from that of visitor to settler while in Australia. Visitors are expected to go quietly at the end of their stay, and the Australian authorities naturally take a dim view of those who try to stay on illegally. Illegals are frequently caught and deported, and failure to abide by the conditions of your visitor's visa may mean that you will be denied any such visa in the future.

Visitor's visas are issued free of charge and generally take only a week or two, although the High Commission and Consulates stress they cannot guarantee to issue a visa by a particular date. Remember to apply for a visa for the full period you intend to stay, since extensions are granted only in exceptional circumstances.

## ★ Working Holiday Visas ★

The working holiday scheme is a terrific idea and an ideal way to see Australia in depth. It allows young people to stay for up to one year and to work on a casual basis. The primary objective of the working holiday scheme, a form of temporary residence, is to foster cultural exchange, and those who are given visas are expected to have an interest in Australia and in travelling extensively in the country.

It is not intended that working holiday visa holders should get off the plane, put their heads down and work away in one place for a year. Keeping any job for more than three months is against the rules of the scheme. Popular wisdom (rather than proven fact) holds that the tax office does not pass on to the immigration authorities information about how long you have held a job, but it is unwise to rely on this. Those who abuse the scheme may have problems with visa applications in the future.

The formal requirements are not difficult to comply with. You will probably be able to get a working holiday visa if:

● You are single, or childless if married, and aged between 18 and 25. (There is a rarely used provision for issuing them to people between 26 and 30 in exceptional cases.)
● You are visiting Australia for a specified period and do not intend to settle there.
● You hold a UK, Canadian, Dutch or Irish passport valid for three months beyond the date you intend to leave Australia.
● Working in Australia will only be an incidental part of the holiday, to supplement holiday funds.
● You have 'adequate funds' to pay for your return air fare and a substantial part of the holiday. (This is generally taken as £1500 for a six-month stay or £2000 for 12 months.)
● You have not previously had a working holiday visa.

You must not arrange work in advance, except on a private basis and on your own initiative. Writing to Uncle Bruce for a job on his sheep station is OK, for example, while blitzing the employment agencies is not. There is also a requirement that you should have 'reasonable prospects' of getting temporary work. This should not be much of a problem, particularly if you are fit, keen and have skills or experience at some sort of work.

The maximum stay allowed is 12 months. In some cases the initial working holiday visa will be issued for only six months; this often seems to happen to people who apply at Australian embassies outside their home country. There is usually little problem about extending a six-month working holiday visa to 12 months while in Australia, provided that you have kept to the conditions of the visa and have enough left in the kitty for another six months.

Obtain an application form for a working holiday visa (form M418) from the High Commission or Consulate, complete it and return it with:

● Three signed recent passport photographs.
● Your passport.
● Bank, building society or other statement proving that you have the 'adequate funds' mentioned above.

Provided you meet the criteria and take care to fill in the form completely and accurately, there should be little difficulty in getting your working holiday visa within a couple of weeks.

## ★ Temporary Residence ★

This category permits people to live and work in Australia for up to four years. It is available for a variety of reasons, and unlike the working holiday visa does not have an age requirement. Among those to whom it is available are:

● Those taking up temporary work in Australia, for example employees transferred there by an international company for a specific period.
● Academics taking up temporary appointments.
● Sportspeople.
● Entertainers.
● People entering Australia to carry out religious duties.

Some of those applying for temporary residence of less than four months do not need an Australian sponsor and may apply on their own behalf, using form M147. Generally speaking, however, to be eligible for temporary residence you must be sponsored by an employer or other organization in Australia. This sponsor must, among other things, make the application for a visa on your behalf and pay the application fee in Australia, arrange accommodation, ensure that you do not engage in activities other than those for which you were permitted to enter, ensure that laws relating to your employment are observed, and be responsible for your departure.

The spouse or children of a person granted temporary residence will not be permitted to work, and you may be subject to health and character checks before you are granted temporary residence.

## ★   Student Entry   ★

Provisions are made for students to enter Australia to pursue a course of study. There are three entry categories:

● Full fee, for which the student bears all the fees and living expenses.
● Subsidy, fees for which are paid in part by the student (Overseas Student Charge or OSC, about 55%).
● Sponsored, which is aimed mostly at developing countries and is part of Australia's foreign aid programme.

All students must complete a student application form (form N) and a visa application form (form M157) and must usually undergo medical and X-ray examinations. The High Commission or Consulate can supply detailed information, but the general requirements are that you must:

● Be applying for full-time study.
● Be academically qualified for your proposed course.
● Have an adequate standard of English.
● Have the capacity to cover all expenses during your entire stay in Australia.
● Be genuinely seeking temporary entry to study only.
● Be of good health.

Students are expected to leave Australia after their period of study or training, and applications by subsidized overseas students to return to Australia as permanent residents (see below) will not normally be considered within two years of their departure after study.

There are also a number of student exchange schemes, usually aimed at promoting international understanding through widening cultural horizons or providing work experience. For these there are separate visa arrangements based on reciprocal agreements between countries. Organizations such as Rotary International, American Field Service (AFS), the International Association for the Exchange of Technical Students (IAESTE), Youth for Understanding and GAP (Activity Projects Post-school) arrange a variety of exchange schemes. There are also institution-to-institution schemes for transfer and exchange at all levels, especially tertiary.

Since 1 March 1989, Medicare cover has been stopped for full fee students, occupational trainees and their dependants. Instead, an overseas student health cover plan, OHSC, has been introduced. This is managed by Medibank, the private health insurance company. Before being granted their temporary entry permits, students will have to enrol in this scheme and pay a premium to cover their period of authorized stay in Australia.

## ★   Migration   ★

Migrating to Australia is a whole new kettle of possums – rather more complex and difficult than going as a visitor, working holidaymaker or temporary resident. Far more people want to go to Australia than the country permits to enter: in recent years there have been ten applications for each of the 140,000 places available annually. This tide of potential migrants is channelled through a number of categories to select the people best equipped for life in Australia and likely to be of most benefit to the country.

Australia's newly updated migration policy is global and non-discriminatory. It lays down the number of migrants from all parts of the world who will be accepted in a given year. There is no set quota for a particular country; instead, migrants qualify by having relatives in Australia or by being prepared to bring in needed skills, experience or capital.

## POLICY REVIEW

Migration has always been an important feature of Australian life, vital to its development, but often also a source of controversy. Migration policy is kept under review by Australian governments and has gone through continuous change over the years. The latest revamp of procedures was on 1 July 1989, when new categories and new methods of selection were introduced. Since this is a new and untried system there are likely to be ongoing changes to fine-tune the selection process.

When you first enquire about migration to Australia the High Commission or Consulate will send you a preliminary enquiry form (form M802) together with some explanatory leaflets. These cover the categories of migration, the requirements, the procedures for applying and the likelihood of being successful. Read all this information carefully to discover whether it is worth your while applying.

There are three principal components in Australia's new programme:

- Special Eligibility Migration.
- Family Migration.
- Economic Migration.

Each of these has different categories within it, and each has its own special requirements.


## SPECIAL ELIGIBILITY

This covers 'people who would represent a demonstrable gain to Australia or who have a close association with Australia'. The phrase, from the official literature, is intended to include outstanding sports, arts and scientific figures on the one hand, and on the other the dependants and spouses of New Zealand citizens and former citizens or permanent residents of Australia who have lost their citizenship but maintained close links with Australia. Australia also makes provision to take in others: those who want to retire to

Australia and have relatives there, refugees, displaced persons and people seeking entry on humanitarian grounds. All of these areas are quite specialized and will not be dealt with at length here.

The vast bulk of migration to Australia takes place under the headings of Family Migration and Economic Migration. Of these two, Family Migration is by far the more common, as its requirements are easier to meet than those for Economic Migration.


FAMILY MIGRATION

Under this heading, there are two categories:

● Preferential Family Migration.
● Concessional Family Migration.

The Preferential category is for close relatives and fiancé(e)s of people who are either citizens or permanent residents of Australia. If you are the spouse, fiancé(e) or unmarried child (under the age of 18) of your sponsor you are eligible under this category. You are also eligible if you are a parent, half or more of whose children are living legally in Australia (the Balance of Family rule), or if in your family you are the last remaining brother, sister or non-dependent child outside Australia.

Your sponsoring relative must undertake to provide accommodation and financial support for you in Australia and, unless you are the spouse, fiancé(e) or dependent child of your sponsor, the sponsor must have been a legal permanent resident or citizen of Australia for two years or more.

Preferential Family is probably the most straightforward migration category. Qualifying is a matter of proving your relationship with your sponsor and the sponsor's ability to fulfil his or her duties.

Concessional Family Migration is for more distant relatives than those mentioned above: non-dependent child, parent not qualified under the Balance of Family rule, brother, sister, nephew or niece of the sponsor. In addition to this sponsorship requirement, those applying under Concessional Family Migration must pass the Points Test, which is outlined below.


## ECONOMIC MIGRATION

This heading is the one under which Australia accepts people who will be of most use to the country in filling shortages in Australia's labour market or in developing business in the country. It contains four categories, each with different criteria:

- Tripartite Negotiated Arrangements: skilled people under 55 who are nominated by an employer in Australia as part of an industry-wide agreement with the government on skill shortages.
- Employer Nomination Scheme: skilled people under 55 who are nominated by an Australian employer outside the framework of a Tripartite Negotiated Arrangement.
- Business Migration Programme: people who have a successful background in business and who wish to set up a substantial business in Australia and have $500,000 in capital for this purpose.
- Independent: skilled young people who are able to pass the Points Test detailed below.

The first two categories, Tripartite Negotiated Arrangements and Employer Nomination Scheme, are relevant for people who have skills which are very much in demand in Australia. An employer must go to a good deal of trouble to nominate an applicant and demonstrate that this position cannot be filled by an Australian. Naturally, an employer will do this only for people of whom he has a pressing need.

There are a wide range of skills, trades, crafts and professions which may enable you to be accepted for migration under these categories by getting an Australian employer to nominate you. The Occupation Shortage List which accompanies the Points Test below is one indication of jobs in sufficiently high demand to justify nomination. Employers who advertise jobs in British newspapers are also likely to be

19

willing to go through nomination. If you have such a skill, the nominating employer will guide you through your end of the application process. Your trade or professional qualifications must be acceptable in Australia for your application to succeed.

The nomination must meet the following requirements:

- The job offer must be genuine, and not just intended to help someone migrate.
- The vacancy must be for full-time, permanent employment.
- The position must be highly skilled.
- The terms and conditions of employment must not be less than the current market levels in Australia.
- The employer must have a 'satisfactory training record'.
- The employer must have tested the labour market by advertising the job widely, and must be able to defend the decision to seek someone to fill it from overseas.

Business Migration, the third category, makes substantial demands of the applicant – requiring capital of $500,000 as well as a successful business background. However, if you meet these criteria you will get every official assistance with your application, since Australia is very keen to admit budding Murdochs and Bonds. If you meet the main criteria, make an appointment with the Business Migration Programme officer at the High Commission or Consulate and they will explain the programme in detail. All Australian states are anxious to have successful businesses located in them, and their UK offices will be able to help with your plans for migration.

Independent Migration, the fourth category for Economic Migration, is the one on which very many young people keen to migrate to Australia depend. Its main requirement, passing the Points Test, is less clear-cut than, for example, having a close relative in Australia, or having $500,000 to bring with you. Therefore it is important to look honestly at how you match the requirements before you decide to apply under it.

# ★ The Points Test ★

This is a selection procedure within the Concessional Family and Independent Economic categories, designed to pick those people best suited for life in Australia and who are likely to be of most benefit to the country. Points are awarded for factors such as employability, language skills and age. These categories are straightforward enough, but the test is made devilishly complicated by having several different pass marks, depending on the category of the application.

Gaining 'priority marks' means that you are accepted for migration. If you do not reach the priority mark, but reach the 'pool entrance mark', you are included in a reserve pool of applicants. Applicants who do not reach the pool entrance mark are rejected. Applicants who make it into the pool wait for a 'floating pass mark' announced twice a year by the Australian Government. When this mark is announced, in November 1989 and March 1990 for example, those in the pool who have points equal to this floating pass mark are accepted. You get three tries for the floating pass mark, after which your application will be thrown out of the reserve pool. It is highly unlikely that the floating pass mark will be brought down substantially, as it will be governed by the number of places left overall in the Independent Economic and Concessional Family Migration programme.

These are the priority and pool entrance marks for the two categories to which the points test applies:

|  | Concessional Family | Independent Economic |
|---|---|---|
| Priority Mark | 105 | 110 |
| Pool Entrance Mark | 85 | 95 |

## CHECK YOUR POINTS

Both Concessional Family and Independent Economic categories earn points for employability and age. To these points Independent applicants add points for language skills. Concessional applicants add points for factors like relationship,

citizenship, settlement and location relating to the sponsor.
So get out your pencil and check your points.

## EMPLOYABILITY FACTOR
*(Concessional Family and Independent Economic)*

| 1. Skill – occupations requiring: | Points |
| --- | --- |
| Trade certificate/degree (acceptable in Australia) with sound, continuous relevant experience, included on the Occupation Shortage List (see below) | 75 |
| Trade certificate/degree (acceptable) with sound, continuous relevant experience | 70 |
| Trade certificate/degree (acceptable) without experience | 60 |
| Diploma (acceptable) with sound, continuous relevant experience | 45 |
| Diploma (acceptable) without experience | 40 |
| Trade certificate/degree/diploma (recognized outside Australia and requiring only minor upgrading – which must be available in Australia) with sound, continuous, relevant experience | 35 |
| Trade certificate/degree/diploma (recognized outside Australia and requiring only minor upgrading – which must be available in Australia) without experience | 30 |
| Other post-secondary school qualifications or relevant experience | 30 |
| Secondary school completion | 20 |
| Four years' secondary schooling | 10 |
| Less than four years' secondary schooling | 0 |
| Never worked | 0 |

● The phrase 'sound, continuous relevant experience' means that you must have worked in your occupation for at least three years prior to the time of your application.
● For a qualification to be 'acceptable' in Australia it must be recognized by an official body as equivalent to that held by people qualified in that field in Australia. There is a formal process for the recognition of qualifications.

More detail on this important point – a major stumbling block – is given in Chapter 3.

| 2. Age | Points |
|---|---|
| 18 to 24 years | 25 |
| 25 to 29 years | 20 |
| 30 to 34 years | 15 |
| 35 to 39 years | 10 |
| 40 to 44 years | 5 |
| over 45 years | 0 |

## LANGUAGE SKILLS
*(Independent Economic category only)*

| | Points |
|---|---|
| Proficient in English | 15 |
| Reasonably proficient in English | 10 |
| Bilingual in languages other than English or only limited English | 5 |
| Extensive English training required | 0 |

● Obviously, those migrating from an English language country may be sanguine about these points.

## FACTORS RELATING TO SPONSOR
*(Concessional Family category only)*

| 1. Relationship factors | Points |
|---|---|
| If you are: Parent | 15 |
| Brother, sister, non-dependent child | 10 |
| Nephew or niece | 5 |
| 2. Citizenship factor | Points |
| If your sponsor has been Australian citizen for five years or more | 10 |
| Australian citizen for less than five years | 5 |

**3. Settlement factor**                                        Points
If your sponsor has sound, continuous employ-
ment in Australia over the last two years (no
employment benefits for more than one month in
total)                                                             10

---

**4. Location factor**                                          Points

If your sponsor has lived in any of the following
designated areas for the last two years: anywhere
in the state of Tasmania or South Australia; anywhere in the Northern Territory, the Pilbara
region or south-west region of Western Australia;
Queensland except Brisbane, Sunshine Coast,
Gold Coast and Far Western Queensland               5

---

**OCCUPATION SHORTAGE LIST** *(relevant to top score for skill
in Concessional Family and Independent Economic categories)*

| Occupation | Qualification |
| --- | --- |
| Electronic Engineer | Degree |
| Industrial Engineer | Degree |
| Quantity Surveyor | Degree or Diploma |
| Computing Professional | Degree or Diploma |
| Accountant | Degree or Diploma |
| Nurse | Degree or Diploma or hospital-based certificate |
| Physiotherapist | Degree |
| Occupational Therapist | Degree |
| Speech Pathologist | Degree |
| Radiographer (Diagnostic) | Diploma |
| Tool and Die Maker | Trade Qualifications |
| Electrical Mechanic | Trade Qualifications |
| Electrical Fitter | Trade Qualifications |
| Refrigeration Mechanic | Trade Qualifications |
| Plumber | Trade Qualifications |
| Vehicle Mechanic | Trade Qualifications |
| Panel Beater | Trade Qualifications |
| Chef/Cook | Trade Qualifications |
| Waiter | Trade Qualifications |
| Pastrycook | Trade Qualifications |

| | |
|---|---|
| Cabinetmaker | Trade Qualifications |
| Wood Machinist | Trade Qualifications |
| Furniture Polisher | Trade Qualifications |
| Upholsterer | Trade Qualifications |

● This current list of occupations for which there is a demand has been substantially reduced. From 1 April 1989, these are the only skilled people who can get the top score for employability. All applicants in the Concessional Family and Independent Economic Migration categories – and those who had applied before 31 March 1989, but had not reached preliminary approval stage – are referred to this Occupation Shortage List. Previously there were two lists: the Occupational Shares Schedule, for which there was almost automatic entry, and a list of Designated Occupations for those applying in the Independent and Concessional category under the old Points Test. Since policy review there are only 24 trades or professions which will help you get into Australia, from a total of 73 occupations on both previous lists. Of course, the trades and professions on this list will be updated as the jobs situation changes.

## ADD UP YOUR POINTS
Concessional Family Migration

| Factor | Points |
|---|---|
| Employability 1. Skill | |
| 2. Age | |
| Sponsorship factors | |
| 1. Relationship | |
| 2. Citizenship | |
| 3. Settlement | |
| 4. Location | |
| Total | |

| Factor | Points |
|---|---|
| Employability<br>1. Skill | |
| 2. Age | |
| Language Skills | |
| Total | |

## ★ Criminal Records and Health ★

There are a couple of conditions that relate to *all* applications to enter Australia. The country has had more than its fair share of miscreants ('crims' in Aussie slang) exported from the British Isles, so there is a requirement that the applicant be of good character. The local police in the UK are requested to conduct a check on your records, and this must be forwarded by them to the Australian authorities. While minor misdemeanours are disregarded, any criminal conviction is examined.

Health checks and a chest X-ray are required for migrants. This will take place after other formalities are completed, and is the penultimate stage in processing. It can and does happen, however, that the sound from your lungs or the condition of your ears are prejudicial to the authorities' estimation of your capacity to make a full contribution to Australian life. The medical examination takes place at one of a choice of listed medical practices specified by the High Commission or Consulate.

## ★ Fees and Waiting Time ★

Fees are charged for all migration applications. Currently, there is no charge for a visitor's (holiday) visa or a working holiday visa.

Applications for permanent residence cost $5 for the application form (M47), followed by $200 when (and if) the application is lodged – that is, accepted for processing. The preliminary enquiry form (M802), which sets out the Points

Test and gives the Occupation Shortage List is free. You may also expect to pay about £50 for your medical examination and X-ray.

Fees are always payable in the equivalent of local currency, usually rounded to the handiest figure; thus an application form costs £2.50 and lodgement is £100. All payments must be by cheque, money order or postal order made out to 'The Collector General of Public Monies'. You also have to send along a stamp in order to get form M47 delivered to your door (37p in May 1989).

Waiting time varies with each case, and may take longer if there are problems with your sponsor's response or your qualifications. In general, family reunion under the Preferential Family Migration category gets priority. Employer Nomination Scheme applications are also expedited, once the employer has produced all the necessary documentation. Other migration applications can take up to 12 months.

Remember, Australia's migration policy is global. There is no set quota for the United Kingdom or any other country. The quantity of temporary entry visas issued depends on demand, and the number of migration (permanent residence) visas is set for the world each year. Despite considerable political pressure, and an estimated 1.25 million applications worldwide in 1988, Australia intends to accept 140,000 people as migrants in 1989/90.

The requirements are complex, but detailed. Your contribution to speeding up the visa process is to make sure your application is in order. Leaving out information, failing to answer questions or not fulfilling the requirements will delay your application and exasperate those dealing with it. Policy in some consular offices is to return incomplete applications without processing. Gone are the days when some kindly official would simply request the additional information, while getting on with the initial processing.

## ★ Change of Status ★

People temporarily in Australia may apply for permanent residence under a number of conditions. This can happen if they:

- Have been given asylum by Australia.
- Are the spouse, child or aged parent of an Australian citizen or permanent resident.
- Are authorized to work in Australia and are not a student or diplomat.
- Marry or have a *de facto* relationship with an Australian citizen.

People who are authorized to work in Australia – such as working holidaymakers – who attempt to change their status are likely to encounter a confusing situation and considerable opposition. First they must be in possession of a valid temporary entry permit (which includes permission to work) when the application for change of status is lodged. In other words, the working holiday visa must still be valid. Second, they must have been resident in Australia for not less than 12 months. Given that the majority of working holiday visas are issued for 12 months' maximum, the application is likely to be lodged after the applicant has become illegal. This is a mistake, as illegals' applications do not have the full sympathy of the Department of Immigration, Local Government and Ethnic Affairs (DILGEA). (It is possible to apply for an extension of a temporary entry permit, but these are issued entirely at the discretion of the Department, and do not comply with the terms of the working holiday scheme.) Neither can you appeal against a refusal, as this review right (no. 6 of the Immigration Review Panel of DILGEA) applies only to the person who was legally in Australia when the application for permanent resident status was lodged. The situation is confused further by the on-again off-again policy, which seems to vary between States, that working holiday visa holders can only apply for permanent residence from outside the country.

Anyone making a change of status application must meet exactly the same criteria as would be applied to their particular migration category in their home embassy. These include the Points Test, and health and character requirements. There are no free points for being on the spot. The most likely category is Economic Migration, under the Employer Nomination Scheme. Therefore, one must have qualifications which are formally recognized by the appropriate Australian licensing authority. Also necessary is a definite and genuine offer of full-time permanent employment from an employer who has conducted labour market testing and found it impossible to recruit a suitably qualified Australian citizen.

## ★ Permanent Residence and Citizenship ★

People who are admitted to Australia as migrants are given permanent resident visas. After two years, they may apply for Australian citizenship. Specifically, they must have been in Australia for a period which includes 12 months in the two years immediately preceding the application, and for a total of two years in the previous five years. They must also be of good character, speak basic English and intend to live in and maintain a close association with Australia.

It is not compulsory to take out citizenship, but it entails advantages (and requirements) beyond those of permanent resident status, including:

● Entitlement to an Australian passport.
● Entitlement to stand for Federal or State elections.
● Compulsory voting if registered.
● Full welfare benefits for those in migration categories where support was previously the responsibility of the sponsor.
● Employment on a permanent basis in the public service, where applicable (in the States which do not automatically grant reciprocal rights to British citizens).
● Re-entry from abroad without special visa requirements.

Citizens are also protected against deportation, which can happen to those of permanent resident status, though only under certain circumstances. (If, for example, within their first ten years in Australia they are deemed by the Minister of Immigration, Local Government and Ethnic Affairs to be a threat to national security – or if they are convicted of a criminal offence and sentenced to more than a year.) There is, of course, an appeals process.

There is a fee ($30 at present) for the Declaratory Certificate of Australian Citizenship, which is issued after a formal (and by many accounts, emotional) ceremony in which one swears allegiance to the new country.

Those who do not take up Australian citizenship will need a resident return visa to get back into the country after trips abroad. At present this resident return visa, valid for three years, is given out with migrant visas. If you do not take up citizenship within this time, remember to get a resident return visa before leaving Australia. To qualify for an additional resident return visa, you must have been in Australia for a total of two out of the three years immediately preceding the application.

# 2

# TOO FAR TO SWIM
## Getting There

The only practical way to get to Australia from Britain is to fly. Many Australians over the age of 35 have nostalgic memories of the voyage from Europe to Australia, but nowadays almost the only passenger ships calling at Australian ports are luxury cruisers, irregular in their schedules and very expensive.

Over 30 airlines fly to Australia from all over the world. There is competition between them, and they try to tempt the traveller either with discounts or with extras like stop-overs at prices so low as to be almost free.

The one you choose will depend on whether you are migrating, going for a working holiday or just stopping in Australia as part of a round-the-world trip. There are a great many options and things change rapidly, so the advice of at least one travel agent and lots of research are the order of the day. Two travel companies which may be worth checking out are REHO Travel, which specializes in flights down under with reputable airlines, and Trailfinders, who offer all kinds of round-the-world packages.

Among the top airlines flying to Australia are Qantas (the national airline), British Airways and Singapore Airlines. Malaysian Airline Systems (MAS), Cathay Pacific, Thai and Garuda (Indonesian) Airways also operate between London and Australia. They all vary in price, conditions, service, comfort and the goodies they offer as incentives to fly with them. You get what you pay for – the cheaper ones tend to take longer to get there, with frequent touchdowns that they forget to mention when you are buying the ticket. The drinks trolley may be replaced by plastic cups of ready-poured beer, the seats may be cramped – but you could feel that the niceties of flight travel are worth forgoing for a price difference that can be as much as £300.

## ★ Sample Fares ★

There is a complex system of high, shoulder, off-peak and low seasons. For example, this is a current price list for Singapore Airlines for a one-year open return ticket from London to Sydney, Melbourne, Adelaide or Brisbane (Perth is always slightly cheaper): January £1140; February, March £995; April, May, June £895; July £995; August £1140; September £1255; October, November, 1–9 December £1140; 10–23 December £1255; 24–31 December £1140.

These are sample fares only, but several things are clear: the fares dodge up and down throughout the year, and the period between March and June should offer the best deal. If you tie yourself down to going in the wrong month you will get well soaked: avoid September and the week before Christmas in particular. Even so, you are looking at around £800 for a one-year return. Anything under this, or any extras you can get, are a bonus. The fact that your great grandfather could have got there for the price of a purloined sheep is no longer relevant!

## ★ Discounts ★

The basic discounts offered by the major airlines are for Apex, advance purchase and excursion fares. Stop-overs may be limited or banned by taking one of these.

Extra savings may be sought by contacting a travel agent and by looking out for special advertisements in the national papers. Also check out the small ads of magazines like *Private Eye* and the many publications for the Aussie in Britain – *Australasian Express*, *LAM* and *TNT* to name a few. *Australian*

*Outlook*, the 'original and leading newspaper for migrants and visitors to Australia' is worth the 30 pence it costs for the range of advertisements and features it carries on travel, moving and shipping arrangements. It also organizes special escorted flights, using Qantas, if you feel the need of help on the way.

There are dozens of 'bucket shop' outlets in London that offer very cheap tickets, but it is extra hassle to check them. Not only do you have to find a bargain – you have to establish the bona fides of the shop, as some of them sell rather dubious tickets. However, discounted tickets have become more common as restrictions are lifted, and it should be possible to find a reputable agency with fares below the official list prices quoted by airlines.

One London travel company advertised the following fares for April 1989: London to Perth one-way £428; return £659. Another offered Sydney/Melbourne one-way £429; return £730. Watch out for eye-catching ads which seem to offer the best single fares – the returns are often disproportionately high. Round-the-world tickets can be relatively good value – especially if you want to take in several Australian cities, or if you get caught in the high season – as they do not fluctuate as much. A trip from London including stops in Delhi, Bangkok, Sydney, Fiji, Honolulu and Vancouver was advertised at £852. A more exotic itinerary – London; Bangkok; Hong Kong; Perth; Sydney; Cairns; Honolulu; Los Angeles; New Orleans; Boston; New York and back – was offered for £995. The price moves around the £900 mark, depending on the routes, stop-overs and airlines involved.

Addresses for some of the agencies, airlines and publications mentioned can be found in Chapter 12.

## ★  Stop-overs  ★

These are a splendid bargain if it suits your plans to take one en route to Australia; it is a pity to miss an opportunity of seeing more of places like Kuala Lumpur or Singapore than their airports. An example of what's on offer is the Singapore

Airlines deal giving a twin-share room in a leading Singapore hotel, with breakfast, for just £10 per person. This also includes free transfers, a free sightseeing tour, and discount vouchers for car hire and shopping. Bangkok stop-overs start at £18 per person per night, and include the same discounts and vouchers, with the pleasures of an 'American breakfast' thrown in.

Both these cities offer excellent cheap shopping, including (due to their lax or non-existent copyright laws) bargain versions of status symbol watches and other yuppie toys. Unfortunately these often do not live up to their genuine counterparts in performance. If you can bear to be party to doing your favourite millionaire rock star out of a few quid, you can buy cassettes for a quarter of the high street price, or less. They are pirated, of course, and while the sound quality is usually OK, the tape itself tends to stretch and fall apart.

You do not need vaccinations for the two stop-overs mentioned above, and visas are only required for stays of two weeks and over. If a stop-over is part of your plans, ask about them on your first visit to the travel agent – otherwise you may get a bargain fare with no stop-overs allowed.

## ★  Flights  ★

The flight to Australia is fairly gruelling. Depending on stops and transfers, it varies around the 20-hour mark. To keep you happy during the trip, the airlines shove food and drink into you at every opportunity on the way out. They are a bit more restrained on the way back, as you are flying through the night (in so far as there is ever a night in the topsy-turvy situation of flying halfway around the world).

If you require any special food, such as vegetarian meals, make sure the request goes with your booking and remind the hostesses when you get on the plane. Otherwise, vegetarians may end up with a fistful of peas whipped off the plates of other passengers and a dog-eared cheese sandwich.

There is little else to do but drink and watch the awful films (super-sanitized, so as not to offend anyone). How much of the free drink you lap up depends on your constitution really, but bear in mind the hassles that await you at the far end. Do not be disconcerted if the passengers give the pilot a round of applause after you land in Australia. It's not that they never expected to make it – it's an Australian tradition.

Most European flights arrive at ungodly hours of the morning, but the airport authorities are kind enough to keep you occupied for the best part of an hour at least. First, you must remain in your seat while people get on and spray the entire plane and the passengers with aerosols. Far from being a sign that they suspect you all of being lousy, this is to kill disease-carrying insects that may have stowed away in the cabin. Passport and customs checks usually involve queues and more queues.

If you do not have a friend kind or crazy enough to come and fetch you from the airport between 3 a.m. and 5 a.m. (landing on a Saturday may help here), you will probably just have to sit it out until a reasonable hour of the morning. All major Australian airports are served by airport buses, which are cheaper than getting a taxi. But the chances are you will be in such a state that a taxi will seem like a bargain – at any price. Cheapest of all are ordinary city buses that pass through the airport.

The standard luggage allowance for flights to Australia is 20 kg (44lb), including your one piece of carry-on baggage. You can, of course, pack more than this as long as you are prepared either to dump the excess or to pay a hefty surcharge for it if the airline gets sticky. Some airlines, Qantas among them, double the allowance for migrants going to Australia. Even at that, 40 kg (88lb) is not a great deal, so pack carefully.

Bring plenty to read on the plane, and perhaps a tape player or anything else you can think of to pass the time. As usual in this imperfect world, carry on your valuables and anything you really cannot afford to lose or have nicked. A spare shirt and socks help you feel better at the far end. Loose clothes are best for comfort, and take off your shoes to try and stop your feet from swelling up.

## COMFORT

Twenty hours without a cigarette is a long time for an addict. You will not be allowed to smoke anywhere except in your own seat, unless there are spare seats in the smoking section, so get a smoking seat if you have to. On the other hand, if you are ambivalent about smoking you will get an awful lot of other people's smoke anywhere in the smoking section.

There are spectacular views on most flights for those with a window seat. Those who seek extra leg room should beware of the window seat at the mid-wing exit. There is about six feet of space in front of it – but there is also a large escape shute/life raft where your knees would normally go.

Push for your favourite seat on such a long flight: the trouble of getting to the airport early to ensure that you get it is worthwhile. Be absolutely clear about any reconfirmations or check-ins you have to make along the way. Don't wander off too far in airports where you are changing planes, and remember that the duty-free shops in these transit areas have a captive market and prices to match.

One problem with cheaper airlines is that they may try handing you a ready-printed boarding card, giving you no choice in where you sit when you have to transfer in a dazed scrum early in the morning.

# 3

# YOUR SWAG
## What to Bring

### ★ Referees and Contacts ★

You need referees for almost every rental transaction in Australia (even hiring a TV). Get some names and addresses of people living in the area where you intend to live who would be prepared to be your referees. The companies which request this will rarely make contact with the referees – they are only assurance as to your identity. Even if you have no intention of seeing these people, their presence and status in a society in which you are an alien will help. British referees, no matter how impressive, are too remote to be of much use to these companies.

Bring as many addresses of possible useful contacts as you can get hold of, too, especially people working in similar fields. Most people will help a fellow traveller or new arrival, even if it is only to give advice over the phone.

### ★ Certified Copies of Qualifications ★

Photocopies of *all* professional qualifications are generally unacceptable in Australia without certification. This applies more to the State organizations with which you may have to register than to private employers. You have a choice: bring originals of all documents relating to your trade training, skills, educational and professional qualifications and take care of them, or have your photocopies certified (migrants bring originals). Certification can be done by a Justice of the Peace or Notary Public in Australia. There is not usually a charge: all they do is affix a stamp to say they are genuine. It would be far easier to have your copies stamped by the organization involved (university or whatever) before you leave. If this is not possible, a letter from the relevant organization stating your course of study and qualification should suffice. Go to the student records office.

## ★ Curriculum Vitae ★

Bring a few copies of your curriculum vitae (also known as CV, work history or resumé), but it is better to have a new one typed with your Australian phone number and address. It may also be useful to give more information about the nature of your work and experience than you would in the UK, as Australian employers may be unfamiliar with the terms used in your job description and the companies or organizations you mention. Research the Australian terminology in your field (perhaps just by looking at job ads). If your address will change frequently, arrange it so typed labels may be stuck over the old one, or have it all retyped.

Typing can be done quickly and professionally by any secretarial agency in Australia – use the Yellow Pages. ($12–18, depending on length.)

## ★ Other Useful Documents ★

Here follows a list which may or may not apply to you. Where possible, bring originals.

● Work references.
● All certificates and diplomas related to education and training.
● Addresses and phone numbers of British-based work referees.
● Addresses and phone numbers of Australian referees and contacts.

- Driving licence.
- Birth certificate.
- Marriage licence.
- Private medical insurance policies (BUPA etc.); ditto personal, car and household insurance policies. (It should be possible to find a company which makes reciprocal arrangements for these, or at least offers a transfer arrangement for no-claims bonuses or qualifying periods of payment before becoming eligible for cover.)
- Vaccination certificates.
- Prescription for contact lenses or glasses.
- People with special medical problems (e.g. diabetes) or who need special medication should bring the necessary doctor's notes and perhaps the name and address of a specialist in Australia.
- Bank statements. Also bring any credit references which will help you to establish credit in Australia. If you are leaving funds in the UK take a statement of these; also make sure you have receipts for any assets you have already transferred, such as bank accounts you have opened.
- Finally, don't forget your passport.

## ★ Recognition of Qualifications ★

As standards of education and training vary from country to country, your qualifications may not be officially accepted or recognized as adequate in Australia. To be recognized in a particular profession or trade, you have to be acceptable for membership of the relevant professional or trade organization. You also often have to register with or be licensed by a State authority (Registration Board). Registrable or licensed professions or trades include most medics and paramedics, teachers, plumbers and electricians. Innumerable professionals, including librarians, engineers, social workers, quantity surveyors and accountants, need recognition through membership of a professional association.

This is obviously most important when, as with nurses or teachers, you may not practise your profession in State-run institutions without registration (private employers may not be as fussy, or may simply assume that your qualifications are valid). But professional and trade organizations tend to be disinclined to welcome overseas competition to their membership; there is a distinct whiff of unfair protectionism about their refusal to accept holders of some foreign qualifications as adequately trained for the relevant job in Australia.

Before you leave home, you can check with the Australian High Commission or Consulate your status and the steps you may need to take. Of course, for most categories of migrants this will be done automatically, as it will affect their applications. They complete a formal Assessment of Qualifications form, which is then referred to the relevant agency in Australia. The situation is complicated by the fact that there is no one agency governing qualification recognition. The Commonwealth Council on Overseas Professional Qualifications (COPQ), which is based in Canberra, liaises with the professional organizations.

Trades qualifications are assessed by the Trades Committee of the Department of Industrial Relations (DIR). Local Trades Committees in the State capitals assess qualifications and run trade tests. You may have to sit a special oral or written exam, or study and 'upgrade' in Australia. Waiting time for assessment of qualifications, or further exam arrangements, can be lengthy.

If you are not migrating, but a working holidaymaker who intends to work at your trade or profession on a casual basis, the High Commission or Consulate is unlikely to be able to help with assessment of your qualifications, as the timescale involved renders formal processes of assessment impracticable.

Inside the country, the first step should be to join, or simply apply for recognition from, the appropriate professional or trade association. They will tell you if you have to register as well. If you run into difficulties, make enquiries from COPQ. Do watch out for this problem – even some highly regarded British qualifications are unacceptable in Australia. Requirements for States often vary slightly; but generally, if you have managed to register in one State, the others will accept you too.

Nurses may write directly to Canberra for an Assessment of Qualifications form, have it completed by their place of training in the UK, return it for endorsement and have it sent back to them before they leave. The relevant body is: Australian Nursing Assessment Council, PO Box 390, Kingston, ACT 2604. COPQ's address is: Council on Overseas Professional Qualifications, PO Box 1407, Canberra ACT 2601. Or COPQ, Commerce House, corner Brisbane Avenue and Macquarie Street, Barton ACT 2600.

## TRADES QUALIFICATIONS

Sometimes tradesmen will have to satisfy further trade test requirements before they can be accepted as fully licensed tradesmen. For some areas of work in the plumbing and electrical trades, you need a licence issued by the relevant State or Territory Authority. The address for qualification assessment is: Trades Committee, DIR, Level 10, 15 Castlereagh Street, Sydney, NSW 2000. Bring your tools with you: buying good new ones will cost a fortune. If they are heavy and bulky, send them surface.

## ★ Clothes ★

This is not an exhaustive list, but ideas based on experience. Bear in mind the kind of work you intend to do, and the climate where you are going to live. A reasonably smart outfit will be useful for interviews and for job and flat hunting. If you intend to be a waiter/ress, black trousers/skirt, white shirt/blouse and black or white shoes would be handy.

Cheap light summer clothing and underwear are better quality and cheaper in Britain, shoes likewise. All cheap shoes in Australia are synthetic and short-lived. Don't forget *some* warm clothes – at least one heavy sweater, trousers and a weatherproof jacket. It does rain in every major city; Melbourne and Tasmania especially have cold, wet winters. Cotton sweatshirts are very useful for chilly evenings in

41

warmer places. Buy cotton and natural fabrics in preference to synthetic ones: they are more comfortable in hot weather and easier to look after. At the same time don't overload with clothing, as your mobility is important. Everything you can buy here can be bought there. Unless you are migrating, or prepared to drag heavy luggage around, travel light and buy as you go.

## WHAT PEOPLE WEAR IN AUSTRALIA

To generalize hugely, female work clothes in Australia are reasonably smart (dresses, suits, blouses and skirts). Women still wear very traditional 'feminine' clothes to work. Jeans and trousers are not so common, but minis, sexy slits and skimpy sun-dresses are noticeably more popular.

Male work clothes tend to be more casual, with trousers (not jeans) and short-sleeved shirts the norm. Suits are rarely worn, except in the upper levels of conservative businesses. Ties are not obligatory, but make a surprisingly good impression. In summer, men sometimes wear knee-length socks, plain long shorts, light shoes, shirt and tie. This looks cute and schoolboyish, but is not popular with the under-40s.

Casual clothes are exactly that. Standard leisure wear is shorts or tracksuit pants and T-shirt for both men and women. Flip-flops (thongs) are also common. Many bars use 'No shorts, no thongs' as a means of restricting entry – shows how popular they are!

Followers of fashion will find clothes and styles old-fashioned, or just different. This is because the season there is either a year ahead or a year behind the season here, and what you have seen in the shops all last summer will reappear all next summer in Australia.

Suggested list for a minimal wardrobe:

WOMEN

- Suit (perhaps), skirts, blouses (work clothes)
- 2 summer dresses
- 2 pairs trousers, 1 pair jeans
- 1 pair shorts, some T-shirts, 2 sweatshirts

- 1 rainproof jacket
- 1 wool jersey
- 1 smart outfit
- 2 pairs smart shoes
- 2 pairs sandals
- 1 pair walking shoes/runners
- Underwear
- Swimming costume
- Tracksuit

## MEN

- Jacket, shirts, trousers, ties (work clothes)
- 2 pairs light trousers, 1 pair jeans
- 1 pair shorts, some T-shirts, sweatshirts
- 1 rainproof jacket
- 2 jerseys (useful for work if cold)
- 1 suit or smart outfit
- 2 pairs shoes
- 1 pair sandals (flip-flops are cheaper and cooler)
- 1 pair walking shoes/runners
- Underwear
- Swimming trunks
- Tracksuit

## ★ Personal Gear ★

A sleeping bag or bedclothes of some kind will definitely be needed, both for holidays and for your own accommodation. Bedlinen, blankets and continental quilts (dunas) are more expensive in Oz; sleeping bags are similar in price. Beware of cheap chainstore bags, which can be too light, and shrink. The authorities recommend that migrants, especially ones with families, send bedding by air to help set up a home.

A radio cassette player can be useful in the first lonely days. It can help you get acclimatized to the ads, shops and language. Don't forget a few of your favourite tapes. Cassettes cost about $15, and while the range is similar to here they have probably never heard of your very favourite band.

A travelling iron may be a worthwhile investment to make you less crumpled for that first interview.

Apart from the convenience of having these items with you from day one, electrical goods are slightly more expensive in Australia, with a bottom-of-the-range radio cassette player about $120, and an iron $50. Of course, secondhand items are far cheaper (e.g. iron $10) and junk shops abound, especially in areas with a large transient population. Be careful, however, if you intend buying duty-free en route, since some airports replace any duty discount with an inflated profit margin of their own.

Australia's electrical supply is 240 volts AC, the same as Britain, so check that duty-free purchases are suitable for this voltage. The television system is different, so it is not possible to bring your own set. Australian electrical plugs are quite different from British ones, so cut the plugs off any appliances you are bringing.

One item of almost unlimited usefulness is a Swiss army-style knife. A good one can be your instant toolkit for changing plugs, extracting mashed tapes from cassette players and all sorts of minor household jobs. In your bare new flat, it means you will never be without a sharp knife, a tin opener or, of course, a corkscrew.

If you are going away for some time, perhaps to settle, think about sentimental items. Photos, personal mementoes and knick-knacks of which you are particularly fond may seem silly and unnecessary additions to your luggage, but their value will increase with distance and time.

## ★  Vaccinations, Quarantine and Customs  ★

### VACCINATIONS AND HEALTH PRECAUTIONS

Travellers to Australia may be required to undergo a medical check on arrival. Those with suspected infectious diseases are isolated and placed in quarantine accommodation. New arrivals must report to a quarantine office if they suffer from illness or disease within 14 days. You will be given a slip of paper about this when you arrive.

You do not need any vaccinations for entry to Australia unless within six days before arrival you have travelled through or landed at a place in a yellow fever infected zone. For the yellow fever requirement (zones include Central Africa, Central and South America) you must have a current yellow fever vaccination certificate, except for babies less than 12 months old.

Areas where typhoid, cholera, malaria etc. are endemic include most of Asia. Aircraft refuelling stops do not necessitate vaccination, nor do many stop-overs, but you *must* check this with your travel agent. Obviously, if you are spending any length of time in Asia on your way to Australia it is a good idea to have a whole range of vaccinations anyway.

## PRECAUTIONS FOR MIGRANTS

Parents of children under 13 are advised to have them immunized against diphtheria, whooping cough, poliomyelitis and tetanus. If you are migrating with a family this can be done after arrival, at school or local clinics. Similarly, teenage girls should be immunized against rubella (German measles). If your children have already been immunized, it would be useful to bring the certificates with you.

## AIDS TEST

A compulsory AIDS test for all visitors to Australia has been mentioned by the present government. As yet there are no definite plans for its introduction and it seems unlikely ever to come into effect. What might happen if you tested positive under this proposed scheme is not clear.

## CUSTOMS

The usual duty-free allowances are available for goods for personal use. You are allowed one litre of any alcohol (beer, wine or spirits), 250 cigarettes or grams of tobacco, and other goods to a total value of $400 (duty-free). You should keep all receipts. Persons under 18 may only bring in $200 worth of duty-free goods.

Visitors to Australia, resident overseas, may also bring in a variety of other goods so long as they re-export them. You may have to pay a security, or sign a declaration that the goods will be taken out of the country again. Your yacht, car and caravan come into this category. Any unaccompanied baggage and goods are liable to duty and sales tax, unless you are migrating.

## WHAT YOU CAN'T BRING WITH YOU

There are many prohibited goods which you cannot bring into Australia. Obviously narcotic and hallucinogenic drugs are a total no-no. Less obviously, *all* foods of animal origin, including meat and dairy products, are forbidden entry unless given a special permit from the quarantine service. If you have any of the following items, prior approval must be obtained before departure:

- Cats, dogs and other small animals. These can only be admitted under stringent conditions. A prior import permit is required and a period of quarantine necessary. This will probably cost more than your own air fare. Buy a new one when you get there.
- Cultures, organisms, animal semen and ova.
- Live plants, cuttings and bulbs.
- Firearms and weapons.
- Cordless telephones.

Do not bring birds, feathers or poultry products; eggs or egg products; aquatic life or fish; plants, crop seed, live insects or soil; dairy products, including cheese; meat, including salami, sausages and canned meat; fresh fruit and vegetables.

Goods manufactured from protected species of wildlife, including skins, feathers, bones, articles of apparel and accessories such as handbags, shoes, trophies and ornaments are also subject to restriction. Finally, and this is a sneaky one, do not bring food items left over from the plane. Bins are thoughtfully provided for those who forget, or just can't resist those handy sachets of sugar.

The following must be shown to quarantine officials on arrival: holy water; baby foods; nuts; wooden, bamboo and cane articles; furred skins; unfinished leather goods.

## WHAT MIGRANTS CAN BRING

Migrants to Australia may bring in practically all their personal and household possessions, duty-free, accompanied or sent separately, provided they have been owned and used for 12 months or more before departure. This is obviously a difficult one to prove. If they have not been used for a year before departure, they may be liable for duty; these include:

● Binoculars, typewriters, cameras, personal sporting requisites and bicycles (non-motorized).
● Household appliances such as washing machines, refrigerators etc.
● Household linen and bedding such as sheets, pillowcases, blankets, quilts etc.
● Furniture, including pianos, radiograms, television sets, stereo equipment, projectors etc.

## PROCEDURE

On the plane or on arrival you will be given a form to complete. This is a series of questions which amounts to a list of declared goods, if you tick the 'yes' boxes. These will probably be inspected by customs officials. Any items in your baggage may be examined, declared or not. The customs officials are zealous. Do not try smuggling and, if in doubt at all, check with a customs or quarantine official. Penalties for not doing so are heavy: up to $50,000 fine or ten years in jail. A lot of detailed information is available from the High Commission or Consulates; useful leaflets are: *What about my departure? Australia. A protected place; Australian Customs Information, all passengers*.

You can also write directly to the authorities in Australia if you have a special problem. Make sure you get the appropriate authority, as this area is a bureaucratic maze. Some addresses can be found in Chapter 12. Ultimate authority is held by the Comptroller-General of the Australian Customs Service and his collectors at the port of entry.

# 4

# A PLACE TO STAY

### ★ Temporary Shelter ★

Having struggled through the queues at the airport, your first priority must be a place to stay. If you are lucky enough to have somewhere you can stay for a while, use it. Be careful though, if the address is far (more than 15 km) from the city centre. The advantages of free friendly facilities will be outweighed by problems of transport, especially if you want to use it as a base for job hunting and finding long-term accommodation. Do not outstay your welcome. More than a week – no matter how nice you are – is too much for most people!

If you cannot use a friend or relative, all cities (and most towns) have a range of cheap accommodation. Hostels like those of the Youth Hostel Association or Backpackers (with prices between $6 and $10 per night for dormitory beds) provide a meeting place and useful contacts for flatshares, employment and car buying.

YMCA and YWCA hostels are more upmarket and more expensive (around $20 and up for a single room). The rooms are nicer and the Ys often give weekly rates, and have cheap restaurants and social facilities (gym, television lounge) in the building. Some Ys do not mind what sex you are, others allow couples, and a few are strictly for either men or women.

The Melbourne YWCA, which takes men and couples as well as women, is particularly nice, but pricey.

A room of your own, or a locked luggage store, is useful if you have just arrived with all your gear. Use the hostel safe, if they have one, for valuables, and keep an eye on your possessions.

Cheap accommodation, and particularly hostels, gets booked out, so phone from the airport. Choose somewhere central, close to the main bus and rail terminals if you are going to be looking for work or long-term accommodation.

After hostels, there are private hotels. The cheaper ones (about $25 for a single room) are often seedy and close to railway stations. They too, often give a weekly rate, but tend to be less welcoming to the newly arrived. The Country Women's Association (CWA) runs private hotels in some cities. These provide safe, comfortable accommodation for women travelling alone.

Motels are usually expensive ($35 and up, with some saving on doubles) and are often out of the city centre, but they can give good self-catering value to couples or groups.

All airports provide at least some tourist information. Even when the information stand is closed, you can pick up free maps and what's-on guides which contain ads for all sorts of places to stay. A short sample list of hostels and private hotels is given in Chapter 12.

## ★ Long-term Accommodation ★

You have three main choices in this area: renting a flat or house, sharing a house, or living in serviced/holiday apartments. It is reasonable to expect to take at least a week to find somewhere. You will need a street directory (about $20, but worth it), bus timetables, route maps and easy access to a telephone, to help with your search.

Flat, house, share or holiday apartments? Your choice depends largely on your circumstances and on how long you intend to stay. A flat requires a large initial investment of time and money – unless you want to live on the floor and eat tins of beans. Sharing is easier and cheaper, if you don't mind risking strange housemates. Holiday apartments will be equipped and have short leases, if any, but will be more expensive. A selection of sample flat and house prices is on p.56. The rents vary with the season, exact location and facilities offered, so shop around.

Having decided on the type of long-term accommodation you want, pick two or three likely suburbs. Here, advice on undesirable areas and local social life from someone who knows the city is invaluable. Bear in mind transport, closeness to the city centre and local shopping. Most Australian cities are very suburbanized and rely on huge shopping centres which are difficult to get to without a car. Limiting yourself to researching and looking in a few parts of town will make the whole business much easier.

All cities have certain days on which the bulk of the accommodation advertising appears. Usually, it is in the quality morning paper on Wednesdays and Saturdays. Gear your hunt to these days, because the columns can be a bit bare on the other days. Local estate agents will also be useful. Allow yourself a day or two to get your bearings and an idea of rent levels before starting to look in earnest.

Some likely areas that balance cost and comfort are:
*Sydney*: Bondi, Coogee, Paddington and Potts Point in the eastern suburbs, Redfern (cheap but rough). Places like Kirribilli, on the harbour, are beautiful but expensive. Avoid the western suburbs.
*Melbourne*: Carlton, Brunswick and Fitzroy (all becoming more expensive), South Yarra. Anywhere near the university is good for food and shopping.
*Perth*: Subiaco, anywhere near Kings Park, Maylands (roughish), Rivervale, Victoria Park, South Perth (expensive) and Como. East Perth, Balga and Northbridge are good value, but roughish.
*Brisbane*: Quite difficult to find flats here. Many people opt for long hostel stays. Try Kangaroo Point and St Lucia.
*Adelaide*: North Adelaide (expensive), Glenelg, West Beach, Henley Beach.

## WHAT TO LOOK FOR

Try to find somewhere with:

- A telephone. Very useful for job hunting. Employers are not impressed by calls from noisy phone boxes. New friendships are also hard to make without one. Pay phones tend to be few and far between in the suburbs. Having a phone already installed saves time and money. Installing a telephone from scratch will cost five times as much as a simple reconnection.
- Washing machine. It sounds extravagant but will be cheaper than using a laundromat for any length of time. Many places have shared laundries.
- Flyscreens and a balcony. These are not essential, but make life easier in any of the hotter areas such as Perth, Darwin and Brisbane.

## WHAT TO AVOID

Cockroaches: look for signs of these pests and before you move in spray the place thoroughly. (Baygon is a surface spray which lasts for about three months and costs approximately $5). Although relatively harmless, they do infest food and make unpleasant housemates, especially for those from the Northern Hemisphere who are unused to their company.

## ★ Useful Jargon ★

- Unit = flat.
- Bachelor apartment = bedsit.
- Home unit, townhouse = two storey flat.
- Duplex = expensive flat, often with garden (yard).
- Part furnished = very bare essentials.
- Furnished = just about, with beds, fridge, cooker.
- Fully furnished = furniture and kitchen, but usually no crockery, pans, etc. or bedclothes.

## ★ Total Costs ★

You will have to pay a bond (deposit) and at least two weeks' rent in advance. Estate agents will also require a letting fee, (usually 10% of the first month's rent) and Government Stamp Duty (a fixed tax, about $4). The latter two are sometimes ignored by private landlords.

The bond is usually one month's rent. So, for example, if you choose a typical one-bedroomed flat with a gas cooker in Sydney, which costs $110 a week, you will have to pay $440 bond, two weeks' rent in advance ($220), a letting fee of $44 and $4 stamp duty. This adds up to $708. Include the deposits for gas and electricity, about $110 in total, reconnection charges for these services of about $40 altogether, phone reconnection, about $35, and basic kitchen equipment – which is very rarely supplied – at a minimum $25. You are looking at a total expenditure of about $918. This is assuming that you have your own bedclothes. Of course, the $440 bond should be returned, but a flat is still a major capital outlay. It is best if you can find some friends or travelling companions to share the initial costs with. All of these items are dealt with in more detail, section by section.

BOND

The bond should be receipted and registered with the Rental Bond Board by your landlord. It will be returned to you by the landlord at the end of the lease. Landlord and lessees must sign a release form. Some or all of it may be withheld if the property has been damaged. In the case of dispute your property inventory or condition report (see below) will be important. If you terminate (break) your lease early you are likely to be charged a percentage of the loss of rent or the cost of readvertising by an estate agency. This will be taken from the bond. A way round this may be to agree with your landlord to release the bond money in lieu of your final month's rent. To do this you fill in a special form available from the Rental Bond Board and some banks.

## ★  Property Condition Report  ★

Most estate agencies and landlords will produce a written record of inspection stating the condition of the property when you move in. This must be signed by you and returned soon after possession (usually within seven days). Check the accuracy of this, item by item, room by room and if necessary query it. It may be the saving of your bond money.

## ★ Lease ★

Usually six months minimum, sometimes twelve. Read the lease carefully as many of the sub-sections (parties, washing on balconies etc.) can safely be ignored, but others, hidden in the small print, may be important. Make sure you are clear about the notice period you must give if breaking the lease (usually one month or rental period), and the possibility of extending it should you wish to. Your tenancy (period of rent payments and date for vacation of the property) will usually date from signature of the lease, but some landlords may allow you to post-date until you actually move in. This could save a few days' rent.

Your lease will contain standard clauses about responsibility for repair. This will usually be covered by the landlord, but beware of mechanical items such as fridges and washing machines. Sort out who pays the repair man and, if you do, make sure the machines work before you move in. It sounds obvious (and difficult to do if the electricity isn't connected!) but a minor oversight can become a major problem in rented accommodation.

Once you have given notice to terminate your lease, or it is nearing the end of the agreed period, the landlord can show it to prospective tenants. This is embarrassing (who wants prospective tenants viewing you in bed on a Saturday morning?) but unavoidable.

Two copies of the lease must be signed by both lessor and lessee(s) and witnessed. You keep a copy, the landlord the other.

Always make sure you have a lease – forms for private landlords are available from stationers – and receipts for all payments: deposit (if any), bond, rent paid in advance, letting fee and regular rental payments.

# ★ Telephone, Gas and Electricity ★

These should be disconnected (if this has not already been done) and reconnected with accounts in your name on the date you move in. This can easily be arranged by telephone, in advance. Deposits are needed for gas and electricity in some States (payable at the local office, within 7–14 days of connection $50–60) and you will also have to pay a reconnection fee (in your first bill, $20 approximately for gas and electricity, $35 for telephone).

Altogether, you can expect to need about $150 for provision of and payment for services over and above rent and everything else that has already been paid to the landlord or estate agent.

Costs for services are quite reasonable – certainly cheaper than their equivalents in the UK. For example, electricity averages less than $2 a day for three people with washing machine, fridge, tumble dryer, cooker, instant water heater, etc. Using gas for cooking and water heating can amount to less than $1 a day, though this will vary with differing State charges and climate.

Telephone costs, including rental, are approximately $40 quarterly. Local calls are quite inexpensive. The country's size does result in huge bills for interstate calls, and its remoteness means *massive* bills for international calls. An ascending scale, with mind-boggling distances and charges, is in the front of the phone book.

# ★ Dealing with Landlords ★

There is competition for most half-way reasonable flats, and there is a definite bias in most cities against new arrivals and the unemployed. Estate agents will ask you to fill out an application form. Details of referees, bank accounts, credit cards and employment are requested (and given the third degree). Dress and appearance are also taken into consideration. Private landlords will usually interview you with the same criteria in mind. If you haven't got a job, proving that you have enough money is all-important. It may be worth taking a bedsit or rather grotty flat to begin with, while you become established.

As with all flat hunting, speed is essential. Get up early, scan the ads, phone likely places, get the addresses and arrange viewing times. Use your street directory to locate them and visit several. If you like one, snap it up. Be ready with all the information and have enough for a deposit in hand. Around $50 should be enough to secure a place until you arrange a time for the signing of the lease and payment of the balance.

## ★ Sample Prices ★

A sample list of accommodation prices for 1989, weekly rents:

| SYDNEY | Australian $ |
|---|---|
| Bedsitter/one bedroom flat | 100–150 |
| Two-bedroomed unit/flat | 120–160 |
| House | 130 and up |

| MELBOURNE | |
|---|---|
| Bedsitter/one bedroom flat | 75–120 |
| Two-bedroomed unit/flat | 95–125 |
| House | 110 and up |

| ADELAIDE | |
|---|---|
| Bedsitter/one bedroom flat | 50–70 |
| Two-bedroomed unit/flat | 75–100 |
| House | 90 and up |

| PERTH | |
|---|---|
| Bedsitter/one bedroom flat | 65–90 |
| Two-bedroomed unit/flat | 80–120 |
| House | 110 and up |

| BRISBANE | |
|---|---|
| Bedsitter/one bedroom flat | 65–85 |
| Two-bedroomed unit/flat | 80–100 |
| House | 90 and up |

You may find places that are cheaper than these, but they are usually in unpopular suburbs or very far from the city centre. An awful lot will be more expensive. Unfurnished flats are often far cheaper and easier to find than furnished ones. Houses are scarce on the rental market and are always more expensive. Sydney is the most expensive city in which to find accommodation. Melbourne is slightly cheaper, but suffering a shortage of reasonably priced inner-city accommodation. Prices in Perth are rising rapidly and there is a dearth of places in the medium-price range. Brisbane and Adelaide are the cheapest of all, with prices in Adelaide having scarcely increased between 1987 and 1989.

## ★  Sharing  ★

You may find house sharing a far cheaper and easier proposition than having a place of your own. You will meet people and perhaps make some friends. On the other hand . . . they could become enemies for life. If the advertisement sounds weird, chances are the people are also weird. Use your judgement and make sure you meet *all* the people living in the house. In this context 'Broad-minded person wanted' often means the other occupants may be gay. Sources: newspapers, workmates, hostel noticeboards.


PAYMENT

This varies. The ad will say if a bond is required and if rent includes bills. If not, you may have to pay a deposit towards future gas and electricity payments. You pay rent in advance, usually two weeks.

Shares will cost anything from $45 a week upwards. Average payment is $60–80 a week. This works out more expensive than sharing a flat with friends, but you do not have the huge initial expenses of a large bond, equipping the place and reconnecting services. Nor will you be tied to a long lease.

For example, an average house-share in Melbourne, which costs $70 a week in rent, will only require an initial payment of $140 (two weeks' rent in advance), plus a bond if necessary

($280) and perhaps a deposit towards future bills of $100. This adds up to $520, but it is easy enough to find a share which does not require a bond or a deposit.

## LEASE

You should not have to sign one, but find out who is on the lease and its duration. *Do* write and sign an agreement on the notice period needed for you to vacate the premises. This should also stipulate the terms under which you get your bond back, if relevant, and any rent paid in advance. You do not want to end up on the streets – penniless – at 3 a.m., after a blazing row.

## DEALING WITH SHARES

Here, advice is similar for flat hunting. Get on the phone fast and arrange a viewing time/interview. Be prepared for leading questions like 'Do you like loud music?' Depending on the person's proclivities you could find that you are hanged if you do or hanged if you do not.

Shop around and do not get pressurized into taking somewhere. Most house-shares have a stack of people to interview and will call you back having seen them all. Be wary of the ones that have no other applications! Be crystal clear on the system of payment of bills, especially the telephone, before you move in.

## ★ Holiday or Serviced Apartments ★

There is a generic term covering anything from bedsits to luxury apartments. Designed for short-term occupation, their advantage is that they are fully equipped and will have a short lease or none at all. Possible sources are tourist *What's-on* guides, newspaper ads and estate agents. Payment may include a bond and rent in advance inclusive of gas, electricity and other services. You pay a flat rate for all it provides, hence 'serviced' apartments. They tend to be expensive (50% more than a standard flat) but may be useful if you have an uncertain timescale.

An alternative would be to find a hostel with cooking facilities, or a cheap hotel with 'light cooking facilities' (usually a kettle, toaster and fridge) and organize a weekly rate. Neither of these is easy to job hunt from and they are not exactly homely. You will always end up paying more if you stay in one of these places for any length of time. Some examples of these can be found in Chapter 12.

## ★ Cost of Living ★

### ACCOMMODATION

The embassy guide reckons that you will spend one-quarter to one-third of your weekly income on accommodation. Average costs for an individual in a shared flat would be $50–60, but there are big variations between cities, and you will pay less if you share with other people.

### FOOD

Living well, with regular steak, roasts and fish, but using markets and cheap vegetable shops, food should come to about $30 a week per person, or less. Again, sharing is far cheaper than buying for one. Suburban shopping centres and vegetable markets are far cheaper than city-centre supermarkets. Australia goes in for large-scale packaging and discounts for bulk purchases. Half-sheep and huge packages of things are very cheap indeed, but will be almost impossible to use unless you have a big household or a freezer.

Recent figures indicate that the average household (two adults and 2.1 children) spends about 21% of the average weekly wage ($393.20) on food each week. Prices do not vary tremendously from city to city, but fresh fruit and vegetables are obviously cheaper closer to source.

### TRANSPORT

Public transport is quite cheap, and weekly bus and rail tickets are good value for commuters. Many cities have a zoning system with blanket increases for each zone. Regular commuters could expect to pay between $10 and $12 to get to work all week and get around at weekends on public transport.

People socializing at night without a car will inevitably have to use taxis unless they are prepared to go home before public transport stops, which can be quite early, especially on Sunday nights. Taxis are expensive if used on a regular basis.

Most people should be able to live easily and cover expenses on about $150 a week, leaving lots of money left over from the average wage for holidays, eating out, entertainment and, of course, alcohol, cigarettes and such like.

For detailed, up-to-date information on the cost of living, see the Commonwealth Bank's useful half-yearly survey, available from the bank or in the High Commission or Consulate.

# 5

# YAKKA
## Work and How to Find It

After a nasty lurch over 10% in the early 1980s, unemployment has dropped back to a little below 8%. That's still higher than what Australia has traditionally been accustomed to. Unemployment is seen as an important national problem, but there are still a great many opportunities.

On the other hand, Australia is not the land of milk and honey. Do not expect to walk into an easy, well-paid job. Do not go at all unless you have reason to expect that you will get work. There are thousands of bright, educated, skilled Australians to compete with you. You will have to get on your bike and find a job.

### ★ From This End ★

Whether you are hoping to emigrate to Australia, going for a working holiday, or stopping off on a round-the-world trip, you should put some preparation into seeking work in Australia.

Those whose visa depends on having a firm job offer will have to go to the most effort. If a relative can arrange a job for you, so much the better. Make it easier for him or her by supplying several copies of your CV and qualifications. Those who do not have a sponsor to do the leg-work will have to use every avenue to find out about jobs in Australia and put a good deal of work into getting a firm job offer.

A good first step is to visit the High Commission in London or the Consulates in Manchester or Edinburgh. The first two have reference libraries which provide a selection of Australian newspapers with ads that will give you a good idea of the demand – and pay – for your skills. There is also a classified telephone directory for each city. You can gather addresses from these for letters of enquiry. Unfortunately, the Edinburgh Consulate no longer provides a library facility.

Even if an advertised job is not exactly what you are qualified for, it may be worth writing and expressing an interest in similar openings. Use friends, those in Australia and those who have returned, to get information about your field and the likely openings in it. Look up the trade union or professional organization covering your occupation and enquire of it about the situation.

An employer is unlikely to go through the complex procedures and paperwork of sponsorship unless your skills or profession are in great demand. A company may not make you a firm job offer, but instead express interest in seeing you on arrival. If this leaves you with a visa problem, you could visit Australia on a temporary visa to follow up firm openings. If you can afford it, this is one of the best ways of strengthening the interest of a potential employer in you. You will also get a taste of Australian life that may help you to make up your mind on whether you really want to move there.

## ★ Head-hunting ★

Major Australian companies sometimes come to London to recruit people for vacancies they cannot fill at home. Look out for notices of such visits. The Occupation Shortage List issued by the Immigration Department is a rough guide to the fields in which such active recruitment may be taking place.

One of the advantages of being head-hunted like this is that your future employer will often pay your fare and offer some sort of relocation allowance. This is usually set against your period of work with the company: if you leave within a certain period you will have to pay back a proportion of their investment in you. Applying for permanent residence is easier as the company involved will be able to help, under an Employer Nomination Scheme or Tripartite Negotiated Arrangement, so long as you fulfil the conditions.

## ★ Job Directories and Employment Agencies ★

There are other ways of getting in touch with potential employers. One is to buy a job directory of some sort; these are usually culled from the classified phone directories and are lists of companies arranged under their areas of business. If you are too far from the nearest source of Australian Golden Pages to search them yourself, or simply cannot be bothered, one of these job directories may be a good investment.

Find out about the trade journal associated with your occupation in Australia and take out a subscription. If you intend to apply directly for jobs advertised in such a journal, you will have to pay for an airmail subscription – otherwise the closing date for applications will be long past by the time your copy arrives. If, on the other hand, you just want to test the water and see what is on offer, surface mail may do.

There is at least one agency that will list potential employers for you, city by city. Leesons Employment and Accommodation Data Service (LEADS) can be contacted at 4 Cranley Road, Newbury Park, Ilford, Essex, IG2 6AG. There are also some Australian employment agencies with branches in London, such as Centacom (New South Wales House, Third Floor, 15 Adam Street, Strand, WC2; tel. 01–930 5733), or Drake (14 The Broadway, Hammersmith, W6; tel. 01–846 9787). Jobs Down Under is an example of an agency that specializes in arranging placements from Britain. It is a division of an Australian company, Tadmor International Personnel Pty, and its address is 25 Norfolk Gardens, Chapel Allerton, Leeds, LS7 4PP; tel. 0532–681 448.

You could also try Australian employment agencies directly, although they are not likely to respond immediately with specific job offers. The most encouraging outcome is usually an invitation to visit their office with your particulars, after arrival. However, it is worth a try, and a pre-arranged introduction will help to pave the way.

If you are a graduate, visit the graduate careers and appointments office of your educational institution and check the files on Australia. One of the people who work there may have some special contacts in Australia. You could also check with the office in your department whether any recent graduates have gone to Australia. If so, you could contact them for advice relevant to your field of work.

If you know, or even know of, any Australians over here working in jobs like the ones you are interested in, you could ask them for advice. If you work for an international company, enquire about Australian associates, branches or subsidiaries and the possibility of transferring.

## ★ In Australia ★

There are six main ways of finding work: the Commonwealth Employment Service, newspaper advertisements, employment agencies, casual enquiries, friends and contacts, your union.

## ★ The CES ★

The recommended first step is to register with the Commonwealth Employment Service (CES). There should be an office near you, but it is best to go either to the main city branch or to one that specializes in your line of work, if there is one. Check the public services section at the front of the telephone directory.

Register there, giving details of your experience and qualifications. You will have an interview, which will give you some useful advice and suggestions. The CES will then try to match your skills with jobs that are available and will contact you when this has been done. You go ahead and apply for the job in the normal way. In the meantime, call in and check the CES notice boards every second day. Interesting vacancies will come up and disappear just as quickly. The CES is also the first step towards getting the dole.

# ★ Private Employment Agencies ★

Try the private employment agencies too. Find them in the classified telephone directory; they also often advertise in newspapers. The agency will usually ask you in for a short interview before putting you on their books. Here previous experience is all-important. Do your best to impress the agency and its staff will pass on the good impression to potential employers. With large numbers on their books, they will only pass on those people who have impressed them with their capacity to deal efficiently with an unfamiliar company, possibly in crisis, with little help from anyone on the job. This particularly refers to short-term 'overload' type jobs.

Rates and conditions of pay vary from agency to agency. Find out about charges for using their service and whether you or the employer pays. If, as with most short-term relief work, the agency is paying you directly, try to negotiate a reasonable rate. It is not unusual for the agency to pass on only 50% of what the company is paying for your service. The keener the agency is to have you, the better your bargaining position.

# ★ Newspaper Advertisements ★

Find out the main newspaper used for job advertising and the days job ads appear in your city. Like housing ads, it is usually Wednesday and Saturday in the quality morning paper, but, for example, *The Australian* carries a monthly computer supplement crammed with computer jobs. Monday is often good for part-time work. Get up early, or better still, get the early edition, which is available at the paper's offices from about 11 p.m. the night before. You will need time to scan the mass of job ads. Circle those that interest you and put them in order of choice.

Be pushy and get an interview. It does no harm to call about a job even if you are asked to apply in writing. Perhaps you can get a more detailed job description or the name of the person to whom your application should be sent. Maybe you will even be asked to come for an interview straight away. Speed is essential. Get on the phone fast. The hours between 8 a.m. and 11 a.m. are crucial. Be ready to start calling as soon as the office opens, and keep trying. For casual jobs, interviews will only be given to the first few callers, or even to the first person who rings.

## ★   Casual Enquiries   ★

It is surprising how many people find work by simply walking in and asking for it. This is especially true of jobs in the hospitality and catering trades, hotels, hospitals, bars and shops. (Hospitality is the Australian term for tourist and other, similar, service industries – casino, hotel, restaurant and bar work, couriers and tourist guides.) Dress smartly, list the addresses of likely places and set off with your CV and details of your work experience at the ready. Ask for the personnel manager or whoever is in charge of staff recruitment. Even if they have no vacancies, they may put you on to somewhere which has, or keep you on file for future work. Be confident and sell yourself.

You can try this too with longer term 'career' jobs. List the companies that might employ people like you. Write in 'cold' to the personnel manager (call first to get his or her name) and offer to come for a chat. Again, even if they do not have immediate openings, they may keep you in mind.

## ★   Using Friends and Contacts   ★

Here the addresses you gathered before you left home will be a big help. People on the spot should be able to tell you of casual work that is going and companies that are looking for staff. Check hostel notice boards and sound out people you meet in hostels. Strictly casual work that is very short-term goes more often by notice boards and word of mouth than by advertising. A few examples we came across were: packing books in a Sydney warehouse ($80 a day, through a friend of a friend), surveying traffic in Melbourne ($40 a day, university notice board), shifting bricks on a Perth building site ($70 a day, through a friend on the job). Keep your ear to the ground and tell everyone you meet that you are looking for work.

## ★ Trade Unions ★

If the work you are interested in is heavily unionized, like journalism or building, either transfer your union membership or join the equivalent union in Australia. It is worth bearing in mind that union dues may be lower in Australia. Call in to the union office and ask about any service that they have for placing their members in jobs. Even if they do not maintain a file of jobs on offer, the officials may help put you on the right track. Some will even let you use the office as a job hunting base.

If you are a union member and are going into a unionized job, check what the terms of the relevant pay award are. National pay awards cover a great many jobs in Australia and lay down conditions on sick pay and holiday pay as well as weekly or hourly rates.

Union membership is very high and you may find that you are moving from a non-union job to a unionized one in Australia. The closed shop operates in many areas. If you are offered a job in a place in which everyone else is a union member, it is probably wiser to join. A foreigner, newly arrived, is not in a great position for making a heroic stand for the right not to join a union.

## ★ Using the Telephone ★

It should be obvious by now how important it is to have a telephone when you are looking for work. Many Australian companies have an aversion to using the post (even though it delivers next day in every city). They will even send out couriers with messages rather than post a letter. You make it that bit easier for them by having a telephone number, even if it is only a contact number. Agencies are very unlikely to put you on their books unless they can phone you when work comes up. When calling to enquire about work, or answer advertisements, be clear and confident. Remember that your accent is totally unfamiliar to most Australians. Give your name clearly, introduce yourself and state why you are calling. Your telephone manner can be vital: if you cannot make yourself understood, you will not get the job.

## ★ The Junior System ★

Age is very important for most Australian jobs. Many young people leave school (some at 15) and go straight on to the jobs market. Rates of pay, related to age, are set out in some union pay awards. 'Junior' is often specified in job ads and means that the job will go to a young person and will be paid at the lower junior rate. Unless you are sure your talents are so dazzling that you can persuade the company to make an adult job of it, forget it.

## ★ Interviews ★

There are commonsense rules for interviews all over the world . . . be on time, be prepared, bring references and examples of your work . . . you know all this. Australian interviews differ, though, in a number of ways, some quite startling. First, they are more casual. You will usually be interviewed by just one person who will be quite informal and probably use first names. You are unlikely to come under any demanding rapid-fire questioning, but you will not get into details about the job unless you make the opportunity. This casual attitude is good in many ways, as you get a chance to sell yourself, but do not get lulled into a cosy chat. Be more professional than the interviewer.

Dress quite smartly, but do not overdo it. Make as many openings as you can to talk about the job and your own experience. There will probably be more room to build on this and put it in a good light than there would be at home. For one thing, overseas experience is difficult to check on and the employer will probably not be familiar with the comparative job scene. Make comparisons and contrasts and demonstrate your suitability in terms of experience. Be confident and remember to speak clearly. Your accent and position as a new arrival may work against you. Try to show your familiarity with your area of work in Australia.

Be prepared for some hypocritical flattery. Your qualifications may be 'wonderful', your experience 'terrific', you may be 'just the person' . . . and never hear from them again. This is fairly common in Australia, and is one drawback of the more casual approach.

If you feel the interview has gone well, and you are not offered the job on the spot, it does no harm to pursue it by telephone. Call the next day, and even call again. The employer may have had some misgivings about taking on someone who isn't Australian. If you show your determination you could change his or her mind. Generally, you should be offered the job almost immediately, either that day or within a week. Employers do not have masses of applications to sift through, nor do they waste time.

People on working holiday visas have some special problems at interviews. Remember that you are expected not to keep any job for more than three months. Always bring your passport in case employers or employment agencies want to check that you are actually allowed to work. Lying about being on a working holiday, even if it is not found out on the spot, will muddy the water for working holidaymakers who come to the same employer after you. If you like Australia, though, and would like to settle there, do not hesitate to tell your potential employer at the interview. You may be able to apply for residency while on the job, or to return to it having gone through the processes back in Britain.

## ★ Fair Go ★

If you are offered part-time hours, or a few casual shifts, perhaps instead of the full-time work advertised, take it. It is common for an employer to try you out before committing the firm to employing you. The idea of a fair go, of giving everyone a fair opportunity to make the most of and get started, is an Australian tradition of which they are proud. You are getting a chance to prove yourself – use it. Lay into the work, get to know your workmates and your immediate superiors and learn on the job – fast. Chances are you will be working yourself into a full-time place. Of course, if you are absolutely useless you will be given your marching orders without much hesitation.

## ★ Working Holidays ★

People on working holiday visas are really limited to casual work. This means you should try areas of work which are likely to offer jobs on a temporary basis. Seasonal work is an obvious outlet – see below. Also likely are jobs in catering; hospital kitchens and factory canteens often employ people on this basis. Hospitality jobs in areas which do not have many tourists are not as likely, but you could try for waitressing, kitchen-hand and cashier jobs in restaurants, and cleaning, porter and bar service jobs in bars and hotels. Supermarket cashiers and shop assistants are rarely employed on a casual basis, unless at a particularly busy time of the year like Christmas. People with special skills, especially in word-processing and other office technology, are very likely to pick up temporary work from employment agencies. Receptionists with the ability to handle large switchboards are also likely to get short-term relief work; so too are legal secretaries and accounts' clerks.

Nurses would have no difficulty, either working through an agency or getting casual shifts by applying directly to hospitals. Nurse's aides and porters are sometimes sought by hospitals on a casual basis. Teachers may get some hours of 'supply' teaching (temporary replacement, or subbing). For state schools, this is usually organized by the State Department of Education. For private schools, you can apply directly. If you have a good qualification in teaching English as a foreign language, private language schools are a possibility. Most would demand people with good experience. Both nurses and teachers must be registered with the relevant State department to be allowed work in public institutions.

All casual work will be offered on the basis of experience and qualifications. Waitress, bar and secretarial work will not go to (or be kept by) people who do not come up to scratch with speed and efficiency. People who assume they can walk into a job on the basis of their dynamic personality alone will find themselves severely tested.

## ★ Seasonal Work: Agriculture and Hospitality ★

Seasonal work is mostly available in agriculture and hospitality. It is rarely well paid. In agriculture, for example, it usually depends on how much you do. Nevertheless, it may be useful for those on working holiday visas as it is almost always casual work, either temporary or part-time.

AGRICULTURE

Agricultural jobs may be found in fruit picking, vegetable and grain harvesting and in processing and packing on farms and wineries. Your local branch of the Commonwealth Employment Service should be able to tell you the dates of the various seasons. Possible sources of this kind of work include CES notice boards, newspaper ads and, if you are in the right area, local newspapers. It is also worthwhile calling on farmers and asking. Here, the local shop or hotel may be able to help, but be sure of how far away the farm is. Distances between them can be huge. When working, on-site accommodation or camping is standard.

This is a brief list of some likely areas for fruit, grape and vegetable picking, with approximate seasons:

● Tasmania: apples, March–May, potatoes, February–April.
● South Australia (Barossa Valley): grapes, February–April:
● Queensland (Bundaberg area) tropical fruit, January–April, (Kingaroy area) peanuts, March–May, (Atherton tableland) potatoes and vegetables, something going on all year round.
● Western Australia (Kalamunda, Armadale, Kelmscott and other suburban areas): fruit, citrus, September–October; fruit, stone, June–August; (Donnybrook area) apples, March–May.

● Victoria (Murray River area): grapes and soft fruit, February–April.

Jackaroos and Jillaroos are the Australian versions of cowboys and cowgirls or station hands. Beware of advertisements in country newspapers, and in some of the more countrified city ones, for jobs like these. They require people with the experience, knowledge of the bush and survival skills to get through tough outback life, often on stations that are very remote. Unless you are another Crocodile Dundee, forget it.

## HOSPITALITY

Jobs in tourist resorts may be quite easy to pick up if you are about in the right season. Write to the big hotels in the resorts, and use the CES and employment agencies. Even call in, if you are in the area. Do not make the journey 'on spec', unless you want to see the place anyway.

Among the areas you might try are:

Queensland: all coastal towns and resort islands have a fast-changing population of casual staff in hotels, bars and restaurants. Try resort islands like Great Keppel, Fitzroy and Green. The more expensive, 'exclusive' places will want top-class staff. For really casual work, try Magnetic Island.

New South Wales and Victoria: ski resorts in the Snowy Mountains and the Victorian Alps respectively may provide some opportunities. Among the possibilities are Mt Buller, Mt Baw Baw, Falls Creek (Victoria) and Thredbo, Perisher and Smiggin Holes (NSW). The season is very short, July –September, and the resorts are expensive if you do not have work. Ski resort jobs in New Zealand are said to be better and easier to find.

Northern Territory: Yulara, the resort for Ayers Rock, has several upmarket hotels with casual work opportunities. Guide work (showing people around the resort and handling tourist queries) may also be available, especially if you are pretty. Peak season is June–August.

There are many other popular resort areas. Use your head. Anywhere that is a popular destination for tourists will need people to serve them.

# ★ Pay and Conditions ★

JOB CATEGORIES AND THE AWARD SYSTEM

Payment and conditions of work in Australia depend on job category. This will be mentioned in the advertisement or stipulated by the employer. There are four main categories of job: casual, temporary, part-time and full-time (permanent).

Almost all rates of pay in these categories are based on an award system. This means the minimum rate of pay and conditions agreed between the appropriate union or trade association and employers in Federal or State industrial tribunals. Award rates and conditions will vary according to job category.

Casual work is usually given an hourly rate of pay and no sick pay, holiday, maternity, pension or any other benefits, depending on the award for the job in question. No notice period is usually necessary on either side. There are exceptions, however, so ask. Nearly all seasonal work, agency jobs (both secretarial and nursing), bar and restaurant work and supply teaching will be on a casual basis. Most people on working holiday visas or newly arrived in the country will have this type of job, at least initially. Temporary and part-time jobs are also usually paid on a casual basis, though some part-time jobs are permanent.

Full-time work will have all the benefits and conditions of a salaried job, if it is permanent. If so, the employer may pay above award rates in recognition of special skills, qualifications or years of experience. Sometimes unions and management will have negotiated payment above the official minimum award in a particular company. It is possible to begin work on a full-time basis, and be paid at casual rates, for an initial trial period. After this (usually three months), you and the employer may sign a contract and you will become permanent. Some people work in full-time jobs for years and are paid a casual rate. Try to avoid this: you have little security and may miss out on entitlement to paid annual leave, sick benefit, long-service leave and all the other excellent conditions of the Australian workplace.

A general rule is to accept casual rates if you are looking for short-term work, on a working holiday visa or starting off in a job. If you intend to stick around and want a career, see your employer about becoming permanent after three months. Some companies and agencies, often in less skilled areas, with more casual staff who are not heavily unionized (for example: office cleaning, kitchen work), will pay below award rates. There is little you can do about this other than find out what the official award is and find another job which pays it. You will get this information from the union or professional association in your field.

PAY

This will vary with job category, qualifications, experience, work conditions and perks, agency fees (if any) and, of course, how closely your employer sticks to that all-important pay award. Many awards contain loading for night and weekend work, and other allowances for working in remote areas. For up-to-date figures on your field, check the news-paper ads.

Some examples of casual rates:

● Waiter/waitress: $5.25 an hour but can be paid up to $9 more, with extra for speed and efficiency. There are few tips. Awards are loaded for weekends and so on.
● Secretary/typist: $7 an hour minimum, but can go up to $20 and more, depending on speed and experience.
● Bank clerk/accounts clerk/cashier: Anything from $7 an hour to $12; it varies a lot with agencies.
● Barman/barmaid: $10 minimum an hour; will increase with efficiency and experience.
● Most unskilled jobs (kitchen-hand, porter, shop assis-tant) will be paid upwards of $5 an hour.
● Nurse: rates vary a lot, with extra pay for qualifications, experience and areas of work (maternity, intensive-care unit and so on). There is also loading for weekends and work after 6 p.m. A shift of night duty (10 p.m. to 8 a.m.) may earn $190. Many hospitals operate a pool system, so there is opportunity for part-time work, job-sharing and overtime, as well as working a standard five-day week.

Generally, pay is excellent. Agencies usually charge about 6% of gross pay.
● Teacher: hourly supply teaching and private language school rates are about $20. This varies a lot with qualifications and experience.


MEN AND WOMEN IN THE WORKPLACE

The principle of equal pay for equal work was established by the Commonwealth Arbitration Commission in 1969. Both men and women can apply for all jobs provided they are suitably qualified, and are entitled to equal pay, unless sex is stipulated in the advertisement. This can and does happen, if it is felt only one sex or the other can do the job. It is also sometimes necessary to read between the lines. 'Attractive well-presented receptionist required' is unlikely to go to a strapping Lancashire lad.

Women's average weekly earnings still lag behind those of men, even though 40% of the labour force is female. The discrepancy remains because more women than men are in part-time or temporary jobs and paid casual rates or are in full-time but badly paid jobs. Average weekly earnings in the private sector in 1988 were £283.50 for women and $464.20 for men.

# 6

# THE SYSTEM
## Banking, Health, Tax and the Law

This can be no more than an introduction to a whole new world. While Australia and Britain run on the same basic principles about the rule of law, health care and liberal parliamentary democracy, many of the details are different. Migrants may use the special advisory services for migrants, there are also citizens' advice bureaux in some cities, and public libraries carry a good deal of information about your rights and obligations. The best source, of course, for day-to-day information is the advice of friends, sponsors, work-mates and relations.

One pleasant feature of life in Australia is that Federal State and semi-state bodies are happy to tell you all they can. Most have a wide range of brochures and leaflets covering all aspects of their services and will cheerfully fill in any gaps if you telephone them.

## ★  Banking and Credit  ★

One of your first concerns on arrival, or even before going to Australia, will be to open a bank account. The major Australian banks include Westpac, the Commonwealth Bank, the State Bank of Victoria, the State Bank of South Australia, the Rural and Industries Bank of Western Australia (R&I) and the Australia and New Zealand Bank (ANZ).

For size and convenience it is better to stick to Westpac, the

Commonwealth or ANZ, and preferably one of the first two. They both have a huge number of hole-in-the-wall cash machines scattered across Australia. Having spent years competing with each other with these machines, they decided in 1987 to make their machines reciprocal. You can now use your Westpac card in the Commonwealth machines and vice versa.

You can open an account in Britain before you go. Just get in touch with any of the banks which have branches here. Even if you would prefer to reach the Antipodes safely before parting with your precious hoard, it is still worth getting in touch with them and availing yourself of their advice and information services. The Commonwealth, for example, publishes in-depth analyses of the cost of living in each State: these are comprehensive and usually up-to-date. They also run Migrant Information days at regular intervals in London, Edinburgh, Glasgow and Manchester. Attendance at these sessions is by appointment. If you are migrating, it is a good opportunity to find out about your mortgage and loan prospects. Money is not the only topic – though of course all involved want a slice of the action. A building company, removal firm and Qantas also attend, and are prepared to answer questions of a general nature. Rural and Industries of WA also offer information and advice, including a special package for people over 55 who are retiring to Western Australia. See Chapter 12 for names and addresses.


CURRENCY

Since 1966, the Australian currency has been the Australian dollar, of 100 cents. There are notes of 100, 50, 20, 10, 5 and 2 dollars and coins of 1 dollar, 50 cents, 20 cents, 10 cents, 5 cents, 2 cents and 1 cent. In mid-1989 the Australian dollar was worth 47p. While this varies, the usual rule of thumb is to multiply or divide by two to convert currencies.

On arrival in Australia, you will probably have a substantial amount of money to open your new account. Use this to strike a good bargain with the bank. All the banks compete with packages of accounts, cheque books, cash-machine cards, free banking in certain areas and so on. Collect the brochures from several banks and find the package that suits you best.

Be careful when opening an account that you ask for a statement at intervals that suit you. Otherwise you may end up receiving a huge snake of computer paper once a year, which is of little use for monitoring the state of your account.

## PLASTIC CARDS

Two major credit cards operate in Australia: Mastercard (Commonwealth and Westpac banks) and Visa (State Bank of Victoria, and Rural and Industries). Unfortunately there is no interest-free period on goods bought with Mastercard, so it is to your advantage to clear accounts quickly. There is also Bankcard, issued by the major banks, which does allow an interest-free period but has some limitations on use – it cannot, for example, be used outside the country as Master-card or Visa can.

Whatever type of account you open, get a cash-machine card with it. This means that you can do most of your banking without setting foot in a bank, and many shops now have terminals which debit your account directly for purchases and avoid the need to carry cash around.

It is usually wise to wait until you have a job before looking for a Mastercard or Visa card. The banks are not terribly fussy about handing them out, but they do prefer you to have some sort of regular income. Once you have a credit card, it can be used to address all your accounts with that bank and to swap money between them, get a balance or clear credit card bills.

Australian banks do not issue cheque guarantee cards (banker's cards), a fact that limits the usefulness of your cheque book. Therefore, it is useful to have a credit card even if you have no need of the credit element. It can be used for everything from mail order shopping to dial-a-pizza, car rental to telephone sex services.

It is up to you how to choose to bring money to Australia, but is important to have enough cash to get by until you can cash your travellers' cheques, lodge your bank draft or draw on an Australian account you have already opened through one of the Australian banks' British offices.

One word of warning: interest rates are high in Australia, and credit is easily had. Banks blare their free-and-easy approach to credit in lurid day-glo window banners and will happily let you borrow large sums or run them up on your credit card. The only snag is that they want it all back – plus a hefty amount of interest. So be careful with credit. There is an extensive computerized credit reference system in operation, and getting into trouble once with repayments can make life difficult afterwards.

Lastly, if you are heading off to the wilds on holiday it is worth opening an old-fashioned pass-book account with Westpac or the Commonwealth. Fancy credit cards and cash-machine cards are pretty useless in a town with no bank, as the authors discovered to their cost in Strahan, Tasmania and Magnetic Island, Queensland. In small, bankless towns a local shop or post office will often act as agent for pass-book accounts.

## ★ Medicare ★

Australia has a good universal health care service, Medicare, partly financed by a 1.25% levy on all salaries. People earning under $6698 a year, pensioners, war veterans and widows and members of the armed forces are exempt from the levy. Nor does it apply to income over $70,000 dollars a year. This still means that most people working in Australia, whether migrants or working holiday visitors, will be paying the levy. They must, however, have permission to stay in Australia for over six months to qualify for a Medicare card.

There are Medicare offices in most towns and suburbs. You just visit the office, fill in a form and the card arrives within a week or two. If you need treatment before the card comes, you can delay payment until it arrives or get your Medicare number from Medicare and use the number without the card.

Medicare covers 85% of the schedule fee for each visit to the doctor. The schedule fee is what Medicare thinks the visit should cost; beware of doctors who charge more. The doctor may 'bulk-bill' Medicare, in which case you pay nothing, or, if you pay him, you get back 85% of what you have paid across the counter at a Medicare office – no hassle, no fuss. Just keep the receipt.

Medicare covers specialist consultations as long as you have been referred by your doctor, and also covers eye tests, but no drugs or glasses. It covers public ward hospital accommodation and treatment by the hospital's own doctors.

Unfortunately, Medicare is under attack, both from a Government bent on saving money and from certain sections of the medical world. It is very difficult to have eye surgery in New South Wales on Medicare, for example, as many eye surgeons there will not co-operate with Medicare. As the service is pruned, waiting lists grow.

But you need have few worries about the standard of care in Australia. By and large it is excellent. In some areas, Australian doctors are at the forefront of world research and innovation. Of course, it is still wise to get the advice of a friend, workmate or relative about suitable doctors in your area.

Medicare does not cover dental treatment, and dental care does not come cheap in Australia. Does it anywhere? Visitors should have their teeth hammered into shape before they leave. Those staying longer may want private cover especially for this.

## ★ Private Health Cover ★

There is a flourishing scene in private health insurance in Australia, with levels of treatment cover depending on contributions. These schemes were once a tax-avoiding ploy in that companies paid the contributions for their workers, but the Government has clamped down on this by taxing the health contributions as fringe benefits.

Medical costs can be substantial in Australia, so it is wise to seek private cover if you are not under Medicare. In each State there is a private health organization that has a transfer arrangement with UK health funds. If you are a member of a private UK health scheme, check with the scheme about transferring cover to Australia. The advantage of such a transfer is that there is no break in your cover and you can claim benefit from the beginning. If you are not a member of a private scheme, you will have to start from scratch and will have to pay for some time before you get benefits. For expensive elective services, such as orthodontic work, this can be a matter of years.

Many Australians covered by Medicare decide to top up their cover with a private fund. This allows them a choice of doctor in hospital, benefit for glasses and other items not covered by Medicare. The popular wisdom is that a healthy young person can afford to rely on Medicare only, although this may change if there are further cutbacks.

Short-term visitors can insure before they leave home (ask your travel agent) or they can join one of the special short-term schemes operated by the private funds. Unlike the long-term schemes, these will allow instant benefit.

## AMBULANCES

In Australia ambulances charge fees – like very expensive taxis. While they will not present the bill at the scene of the accident, it will certainly arrive later. Some classes of private cover will pay for your ambulance. Medicare will not. You can insure against a large ambulance bill (they can run to hundreds of dollars) or, in Western Australia, make a small donation to the ambulance service. This entitles you to a free ride.

## ★ Tax ★

Taxation in Australia is a complicated business. Federal, State and local governments all want their slice of your little cake. In the case of the latter two, the stamp duties, payroll tax, motor tax, land tax and service charges are levied by State and local government, the systems and amounts vary from State to State and from town to town within a State. By and large, they will come to you.

The Federal Government hits you with income tax, capital

81

gains tax, fringe benefits tax, customs and excise, departure tax and sales tax. As mentioned, government departments and offices will be happy to provide you with explanatory leaflets and information.

Watch out for the departure tax of $20. Everyone leaving Australia must pay it. Remember to keep the money at the end of your stay or your merry gallop through the airport on the way home will be brought to an unsympathetic halt.


## TAX ADVICE

Income tax advisers (or IT 'professionals' as they call themselves) proliferate in Australia. Have one recommended to you and bring your questions to them having swotted up on the leaflets. The advisers' fees may be claimed against your tax.

You may well have to call on one, as income tax in Australia can be a bit of a minefield. All residents of Australia must pay tax on their income from inside and outside Australia. Those staying for less than six months do not qualify as residents for tax purposes. They, and other non-residents, pay 30% tax on earnings up to $19,500 and the same rate as residents above that.

Income tax in Australia is paid in two stages. On starting a job, you fill out a form. Remember to keep a copy. It is illegal to have two of these tax declarations in force at the same time. Your employer will then deduct tax from your pay packet each week. The second stage comes at the end of the tax year on 30 June. Within two months of that date, you must fill up a tax return (available, with instructions, from any post office) and send it in. The fact that the Federal Treasurer failed to lodge a return for several months after the deadline will not cut much ice with the authorities if you follow his example.

Your tax return must have details of your income from all sources and full information for any claims you want to make for expenses such as union membership or work clothes. You prove your weekly earnings, and the tax paid on them, by producing 'group certificates'. Your employer is obliged to give you one of these. Demand it when you leave a job.

Your tax return is assessed by the authorities and you are either given a rebate or – woe of woes – asked for more tax. Generally, your PAYE payments will cover your tax bill unless you have substantial other earnings.

The PAYE tax rates for individuals in force since 1 July 1987 are as follows:

| Dollars | Tax |
|---|---|
| $5100 and under | nil |
| $5101–12,600 | 24% |
| $12,601–19,500 | 29% |
| $19,501–35,000 | 40% |
| $35,001 and over | 49% |

All pay packets are lightened by 1.25% before tax, to pay for Medicare. If you do not get a Medicare card, when the time comes to lodge a tax return ask for your Medicare levy back.

Taxation of businesses, partnerships and companies is complex and requires professional advice. When there are large sums involved, with leading businessmen and professionals, Australians are resourceful in finding ways around the tax system. The present Government is doing its best to plug these loopholes and the situation changes rapidly. You can write for more information to the Commissioner for Taxation, Australian Taxation Office, 2 Constitution Avenue, Canberra, ACT 2600.

## ★ The Legal System ★

The Australian legal system is modelled on that of the United Kingdom. It grew with the colonies from a system of military courts. Civil courts and trial by jury were introduced in the first half of the last century. In line with the colonial status of Australia at the time, British common law was applied, as were some British statutes. The High Court of Australia was established in 1900. There is also a complete court system in each State, from magistrates' courts up to the State supreme court. The State systems are the courts of general jurisdiction, with powers to decide Federal as well as State matters unless some Federal court has exclusive jurisdiction in the area.

The links with the English legal system remain strong. It is only very recently, for example, that the practice of appealing to the Privy Council as an ultimate authority was discontinued. That much said, Australia has been far more sensible than the UK about overhauling ancient irrelevant laws. Where we often hear of people being charged under some obscure statute, the Australians have replaced many of the archaisms with State and Federal laws that are more applicable to the modern world.

## SPECIAL COURTS

As well as the mainstream civil and criminal courts, there are small claims courts and tribunals in Queensland, Victoria, New South Wales and Western Australia. These hear complaints by consumers against traders, and have a simplified legal format and low costs. Australian consumer law is strong and there is no need to accept shoddy goods or services. In South Australia, the Australian Capital Territory and, more recently, in Queensland, lower courts have been given special jurisdiction to hear small claims.

Other courts, like the Industrial division of the Federal Court and the Conciliation and Arbitration Commission, deal with industrial disputes and pay claims. There is also an ombudsman in each State and at Federal level. Their main function is to investigate complaints from the public about government bodies. They are independent of politicians and can bring their findings directly to Parliament if they wish.

Criminal law varies from State to State, but five principles are common to each system:

● A person is presumed innocent until proved guilty.
● The prosecution must prove criminal charges and it is not the responsibility of the accused to disprove them.
● Accused or suspected people are not obliged to make any statement to the police.

- If an accused is tried and found not guilty, he or she cannot be charged with another offence where the same facts are used.
- The prosecution must demonstrate an intent to break the law.

Legal abortion is available in some States. Divorce is freely available Australia-wide. One facet of Australian law is worth noting. *De facto* marriage is recognized as marriage for some tax, immigration and other procedures.

## ★ The Police ★

The blunt end of the law is the Federal and State police forces. All are armed. You would be well advised not to come under the attention of either.

There are variations, but police powers are generally as follows:

- They may make arrests only on reasonable grounds for believing the suspect is guilty (these grounds may be tested in court), on warrant, or without a warrant under the same conditions as a citizen may make an arrest (generally, reasonable suspicion that someone has committed, or is about to commit, a felony).
- If a person is not legally arrested, he has no obligation to obey the instructions of a policeman.
- The police cannot detain a person for questioning. An arrested person must be brought before a magistrate as soon as possible.
- The police have the right to enter and search premises for reasons which vary a great deal from State to State.
- Individual rights are strongly protected in relation to police questioning. Generally, no suspect is required to answer questions or to provide their name and address. A large proportion of convictions stem from confessions made to police during questioning.

# ★ Driving ★

The main area in which Australian law will impinge on the average law-abiding visitor or migrant is in relation to driving. Bring an international driving licence with you, as well as your British one. It could be useful for purposes of identification, especially with car hire firms. They are available from the AA or RAC for a small fee. If you are on a working holiday, delay getting the licence until shortly before you leave, as it is valid only for one year from date of issue.

British licences are accepted, though if you are migrating you will have to get an Australian licence at some stage, after a reasonable 'grace' period (which is somewhat hazy and varies between States). It seems that visitors can use their UK licences for 12 months, while permanent residents are officially allowed only three months' grace.

To get an Australian driving licence, you must produce your UK licence at the local (State) Department of Transport. You undergo an eye test, either a written (multi-choice) or oral test on the highway code, and away you go – as long as your licence has no endorsements on it. Without a licence, or if it has expired, you will have to take a practical driving test as well. This test is less demanding in Australia than in some countries – visiting Japanese students queue up to get their licences before returning to the rigours of Tokyo traffic. Remember to carry your licence when you drive. In some States it is an offence not to be able to produce it on the spot.

The highway code varies from State to State, as do traffic rules. They drive on the left as we do, but there are some variations. There is a 'give way to the right' rule, which means that if you are driving and see a car emerging from a road to the right you must give way to it. Usually, minor roads are signposted to show who has right of way. But in certain places, like rural Queensland and some residential areas, you must be very careful. In Victoria, there is an extra twist to this rule: if two cars approaching each other turn into the same street, the one turning right has priority. At some intersections in Melbourne (clearly marked) cars intending to turn right must pull in to the left-hand side of the road.

Try to follow someone else's lead, and watch out for the trams. It can be very hard to get off a freeway if you miss a turn, so check out your route in your city street guide before you start. Many Australians keep the street guide in the car.

ROAD LAW

Australia is metric. That includes speed limits and distance signs: the 110 sign is not an invitation to try for the old-fashioned ton. The general speed limit in urban areas is 60 km per hour. On the open road, it ranges from 100 to 110 kph. There is no general speed limit on the open road in the Northern Territory.

The police are fond of setting speed traps and collect large sums of money this way. Part of the reason is the determined nationwide campaign to get the level of death on the roads reduced. Even in the open country police sometimes use spotter planes to catch speeding motorists by timing them between two set marks. Some traffic lights are neatly wired up with beams to detect those who crash the lights and with cameras to snap them in the act. Be careful. The wearing of seat belts is compulsory.

Far more serious is driving under the influence of drink, drugs or both. Random breath testing is widespread. Especially at holiday periods and Christmas, the police work their way through hundreds of motorists. They sometimes even stake out parties and test everyone who leaves. Drunk driving, or DD, is seen as a social menace and in some areas the names of all those convicted are published in the local newspapers. The penalties are severe.

## ★ Drugs ★

Whether in a car or not, the use and possession of illegal recreational drugs can also attract severe penalties. Australia has a marvellous climate for growing cannabis and it is widely used, but the penalties for being caught in possession of it vary widely. New South Wales and Victoria are comparatively lenient on those convicted of having small amounts of it, while in Queensland the punishments are draconian. Penalties for dealing in cannabis and for the abuse of hard drugs are uniformly severe.

## ★ Welfare and Social Security ★

There is a wide range of social security and welfare benefits available. Generally social welfare is seen as a last resort, and most payments are income- and sometimes asset-tested to very low income or savings levels, which include your partner – married or *de facto* – in the reckoning. The system can be abused, but fraud is often detected and the penalties are harsh. In a country with some work to offer, there is no social standing in being called a 'dole bludger'.

Working holiday and other short-term visitors are not generally entitled to social welfare. You need permanent residence status to qualify, though British citizens may get basic welfare payments within the first six months if they qualify on income grounds. Those who have migrated with the aid of a sponsor who has completed an 'Assurance of Support' form are also effectively disqualified – the sponsor is billed for your dole, or any other welfare and pension benefits you collect.

There is no equivalent of pay-related social insurance or 'contributory' pensions or benefits in Australia, since people who are working do not pay National Insurance contributions. Instead, welfare payments come from State reserves and are issued according not only to means, but also to length of residence in the country. Sickness benefit insurance is organized by a workers' compensation system – 'compo'.

If you intend to return to the UK, it may be worth arranging to pay voluntary National Insurance contributions while you are away, to maintain your entitlement to unemployment benefit and State pension. There is a reciprocal agreement in force between the two countries, which covers age, invalid and widow's pensions, and unemployment and sickness benefit, but the whole area is fraught with complications and exceptions. It is worth checking your position, especially in relation to pension rights, with your local DHSS office before you go. Alternatively the Registrar for the Department of Social Security at Australia House may help. The DHSS has two leaflets: *Social Security Agreement Between United Kingdom and Australia* (SA.5), and *Social Security Abroad* (NI.38). Write to the Department of Health and Social Security, Overseas Branch, Benton Park Road, Newcastle Upon Tyne, NE38 1YX.

Short-term assistance available in Australia includes the following:

- Sickness Benefit (asset tested for those over 25).
- Job Search Allowance for those under 18 (income and parental income tested).
- Unemployment Benefit for those over 18 (asset tested for those over 25. Those who left their last job by choice and without good reason do not get it for 12 weeks).
- Special Benefit (a kind of emergency payment when you cannot support yourself: not available to temporary residents).
- Rent assistance and allowances for spouse and children are also available for short-term benefit recipients.

Other allowances include Family Allowance (income tested since 1987), Family Allowance Supplement (for those on low incomes not already receiving government assistance), Child Disability Allowance, Rehabilitation Allowance and Sheltered Employment Allowance.

Long-term assistance includes Invalid Pension, Service Pension, Orphan's Pension, Widow's Pension, Spouse Carer's Pension, Supporting Parent's Benefit and Age Pension. Pensioners are usually eligible for fringe benefits, such as a Health Care Card and reduced telephone rental. The perks vary from State to State, but can include rate and water charge exemptions, reduced electricity and public transport charges, as well as many discounts offered by private organizations.

If you want to qualify for any of these benefits, pensions or allowances the people to contact are the local Department of Social Security (DSS). The head office is at Juliana House, Bowes Street, Phillip, ACT 2606, or you can write to PO Box

4158, Sydney, NSW 2000. The CES are the people to register with for unemployment benefit.

As with so many aspects of Australian life, there is a refined system of appeals tribunals if you feel you have been unfairly treated. You also have the right to see your file and read the DSS *Manuals of Instruction* under the 1982 Commonwealth Freedom of Information Act.

# 7

# SETTLING IN

## ★ Making Friends ★

Australian cities may *look* similar to those in Europe, and Australian people may seem similar to Europeans – but they are not. All sorts of differences exist between those in the Southern Hemisphere and us of the cold North, and the longer you stay the more these become apparent. People use different language, spend their spare time doing different things, relate to each other differently, and may have a different perspective on their place in the affairs of the globe. To make the most of your time in Australia, or to make a happy transfer to living there permanently, you must be open-minded, unprejudiced and ready to learn.

We are all guilty of stereotypes – how many friends to whom you mentioned going to Australia responded with 'G' day mate' and spoke of beer-drinking Aussies, hats with corks, kangaroos, Crocodile Dundee and surfboards? Of course these are features of Australia, even if some are kept going by the tourist trade. The country is so vast, and inhabited by people of so many different races, ethnic origins, interests and lifestyles, that the only generalization you can safely make is about its infinite variety. Super-cliché number one is 'It's a big country. . . .' You will hear it again and again, and even find yourself saying it.

Do not keep making comparisons, favourable or otherwise,

with the 'old country'. Tell people about it if they are interested. Comments on differences are likely to be misinterpreted, and complaints are treated unsympathetically. The logic is, you *chose* to come to Australia. Sounds reasonable enough.

You may be a model human being – honourable, self-reliant, stoical and sympathetic – and admirable in every respect, but being from Britain means that you will inevitably meet a certain amount of usually good-natured flak in Australia. This may include being called a 'Pommy bastard' (which Australians swear is a term of affection) or a 'Whingeing Pom' (less affectionate). It will almost certainly include widespread rejoicing whenever the England XI lose a wicket, and a certain amount of condescension towards the dubious joys of living in Thatcher's Britain.

Very little can be done about this. Relations between colonizer and colonized are always a little fraught – ask an Indian, an Irishman, a Cypriot or even a Scot. And it must be admitted that many of the first Poms to hit Australia whinged a great deal and with good reason – particularly those who arrived in chains. The best thing to do is not to take any of it too seriously, stay calm, and remember how strong links between Britain and Australia remain.

Be prepared for endless questions from friends and workmates about why you have come. People are genuinely interested in you and your motivation. While money and having a reasonable standard of living are obviously important, try to let Australians know you are interested in and appreciate their country. The answer 'To make lots of money, drink beer and lie in the sun' sounds pretty pathetic. On the same note, don't knock Britain too much or let other people run it down in front of you. Australians are patriotic people and proud of their country. Scathing criticism of your own land may well make them think less of you.

## ★ The Myth of the Philistine Aussie ★

Of course there are Australians to whom the height of man's achievement is the invention of beer, whose idea of getting dressed up is to drag a cleanish singlet over their beer guts, and who would sooner eat a book than read one. There are people in any country of whom the same things are true. In Australia, as in any country, they are the exceptions.

The notion that all Australians are beer-swilling louts, whose sexual foreplay consists of the words 'Brace yerself, Sheila' and that all things Australian are crude imitations of those of Europe is utter rubbish. If you entertain any suspicion that it is true, better leave it behind.

Keep an open mind, put in a little effort and you will be richly rewarded by the vitality and richness of Australia – from wine to art and language to music. One sure way to lose Australian friends, or avoid making any in the first place, is to treat all things Australian as 'colonial' and second-rate, or to join up with the whingeing Poms who do.

## ★ The Media ★

Despite having a small population spread over a massive area, or perhaps because of it, Australia is a media-mad society. The media of mass communication have an enormous impact on the life of the average Australian, and in turn these media are the basis of a massive, competitive industry.

There are approximately 538 newspapers, over 1400 magazines, 320 radio stations and 146 television stations in Australia, as well as some 650 cinemas. It has been estimated that 98% of Australian homes have a television and that 99% have a radio. In 1984, advertisers spent nearly $3000 million on advertising in the mass media.

You will probably spend much of your free time on one or more of the products of the communications industry, collapsing in front of the television after a hard day at work, scanning the newspaper for jobs and news of home. So what is out there?

### NEWSPAPERS

You will never run short of a newspaper in Australia. There is a wealth of them, from *The Sydney Morning Herald* and *The*

*Age*, two of the great newspapers of the world, to *The Cootamundra Herald*, which has a circulation of about 2000. Because of the huge distances between cities, there is only one general national newspaper, *The Australian*. The pattern, for the rest, is one or two morning papers in a major city, depending on its size, with one or two evenings and a couple of weeklies. You will be relying on the quality morning paper in each city for job and accommodation advertising. These are: *The Age*, Melbourne; *The Courier-Mail*, Brisbane; *The Sydney Morning Herald; The West Australian*, Perth; *The Canberra Times; The Advertiser*, Adelaide; *The Mercury*, Hobart; and *The Northern Territory News*, Darwin.

By and large, Australian newspapers are bright, snappy and excellent value for money. The papers, and the media generally, will help you get into the swing of life in Australia, getting you clued up on the issues of the day and demonstrating the priorities of Australian life. One of the first things you will notice is the concentration on news of the region, south-east Asia. Events that barely rate a mention in Europe will get careful attention if they impinge on Australia or her neighbours.


TELEVISION

The average Australian spends about 20 hours a week in front of the tube. You would be forgiven for wondering why at times. The TV system, like that in Britain, has two elements, the public ABC (and SBS), and the private commercial stations licensed by the Federal Government.

It is not economic to distribute TV signals nation-wide so the stations vary from area to area. The major cities, or most of them, have three commercial stations (Channels 7, 9 and 10) as well as the ABC (Channel 2) and SBS, which transmits special-interest programmes for linguistic and other minorities.

The ABC strives to follow the best traditions of public service broadcasting, as exemplified by the BBC. It is usually your best bet for quality programmes and mercifully carries no ads. On the other hand, it captures only about 15% of the national audience. Its finances are at the mercy of politicians and it does not get the resources needed to fulfil all its potential.

Commercial TV is similar to its British equivalents, except that controls on advertising and programme quality appear to be much more relaxed. Its staples are soap operas, game shows and news, with films and mini-series. There is an awful lot of advertising, noticeably more than in Britain, and enough to irritate most people to distraction. Worse still is the system by which the audience ratings are calculated and ad prices set. There are 'ratings periods' during which the stations hit you with their very best product, all at the same time, and for a short period. Between 'ratings periods' they can pump out any old garbage they like, and often do.

Among the redeeming features is the fact that these stations have a lot of money to spend on covering news and sporting events. One other plus is that they run late at night, and some of them all night.

But this counted for little with a well-known journalist who said, on going back to Sydney after 14 years away: 'If you have seen American television and can imagine it without its redeeming features, then Australian TV is even worse than that.'

## RADIO

As in television, there are public service and commercial stations. In the cities you will have plenty to choose from. ABC Radio National does very good news and current affairs shows and also broadcasts the proceedings of Parliament, which are well worth a listen every now and again. On the commercial stations though the choice is yours, from classical music to talk-back shows to the usual pop music interspersed with pseudo-American psychobabble, it is all there. Although many British radio shows use audience phone-ins, none has taken it to the lengths of Australian talk-back radio. Here the public makes the show: a constant stream of callers bounce their ideas off the host. It can be good fun and an introduction to the thinking of ordinary Australians, or at least the ones who call radio shows. Some papers list only TV shows, so you may have to rely on weekly supplements of radio listings to find out what is on.

## MAGAZINES

This is an area of wide, almost bewildering, choice. Top of the heap is *Australian Women's Weekly* (published monthly, so figure that one out), which sells over a million copies. There are all sorts of specialist magazines, but unfortunately no excellent current affairs one. *The Bulletin* is the nearest thing. You can also buy some of your old favourites from home, sent out surface and months out of date. *Private Eye*, for example, is sold in this way.

## ★ Phone and Post ★

Australian postal and telecommunications services are under the Federal control of the Department of Communications. They are both highly efficient and service-conscious organizations – perhaps because they are statutory authorities whose charters require them to meet their annual operating expenditures and at least 50% of capital expenditure from internal revenue.

## TELECOM

The telephone service provides a huge range of facilities as well as mere phones. Public telephone services definitely fall short of its high-tech communications facilities, including those available to the private user. Over 85% of Australian homes have telephones – and they are often pushbutton models, with memory and recall functions. Public telephones are being slowly updated, however, and numbers increased. There are three types of payphone: red, grey/green and gold.

Red payphones are most often found in local shops and bars. They take 30 cents – one 20 cent coin and a 10. These are being replaced, as they can only be used for local calls, and you may still find some which cost only 20 cents. Red phones often have no booths or hoods and tend to be in noisy places.

Grey/green payphones are the second most common type. These provide local and STD calls (long-distance within the country, stands for Subscriber Trunk Dialling). Some have been updated to provide ISD (International Subscriber Dialling) and will take $1 coins. Most only take 50 and 20 cent coins. They are fitted with a red warning light which flashes when your time is almost up, so you can insert more money – if you have it to hand – or have time to say goodbye. If you complete your call before the money is used up, unused coins are returned. If you are making a long-distance call, it is useful to insert a heap of coins at the beginning which can then drop automatically, rather than waste precious seconds fumbling for change. This type of phone is most often to be found in post offices and on the street, especially in the suburbs. Watch out for their strange doors which always seem to fold the wrong way.

The most up-to-date of the public telephone service, gold payphones, are similar to the yellow electronic ones available here. A digital display tells you how much money you have left and flashes when your time is running out. A follow-on button can be used to dial another call, using remaining cash in the machine. If you hang up you only get the unused coins. They take all silver and $1 coins. All types of calls may be made: local, STD and ISD. These are the quietest and best value for international calls. They are usually to be found in secure, salubrious places like airports, hotel foyers, bars and some shops. If they are in a phonebox, a sticker to that effect will be on the door.

The code for dialling Britain from Australia is international code (0011), plus the country code (Britain = 44), plus the area code without the 0 (London = 1), plus your number. If you want to call home on Christmas Day, book your call. Everyone has the same idea and an international line is hard to get. The emergency number, for fire, police or ambulance, is 000. Rates for ISD and STD calls vary with time of day, as here. All STD and ISD calls are cheaper at night and weekends, in other words, outside business hours. Special offers are sometimes advertised – look for super-special low rates for the early hours of Sunday morning.

For those interested in statistics, there are about 8 million telephones in Australia, and 99% of calls are handled automatically. International Subscriber Dialling is available to about 180 destinations. Telephone services are available to 230 overseas destinations. The Overseas Telecommunications Commission is responsible for these services, and all public telecommunications between Australia and other countries. You are billed through Telecom. OTC also provides facsimile (fax), leased circuit, audio broadcast, electronic mail and data transmission services. If you want to send information or simply a birthday telegram from Australia there is a variety of ways. Especially personal is the 'imagegram' service whereby for about $12 your own drawing or message can be delivered by courier to an address in Britain the same day. Heaps of glossy information leaflets about these services are available at post offices. Find out about them – they can work out cheaper than letters, telephone calls or old-fashioned telegrams if you need something in a hurry.

AUSTRALIA POST

The postal service is a massive go-ahead, consumer-conscious organization, employing nearly 35,000 people full-time to handle about 14 million articles every working day. As well as providing stamps and mail delivery, post offices sell aerograms and pre-stamped envelopes and a variety of boxes and poster tubes (post packs). Cheap, lightweight and sturdy, these are ideal for sending presents or excess baggage home.

Postage for a letter within Australia is 39 cents at the time of writing. Airmail postal charges are quite high – at present an aerogram costs 53 cents, a postcard 63 cents and a letter (20 gm) $1. It takes about seven days for a letter to get from Britain, though this can vary considerably from an amazing three days to over two weeks. If you are in no rush, surface mail (about 12 weeks) or surface airlift (about six weeks) are better value for parcels.

Post offices are generally open from 9 a.m. to 5 p.m. Monday to Friday. Some General Post Offices (GPOs) also open on Saturday morning. Stamps can sometimes be bought from local newsagents or suburban delis – they will have a sign to that effect. Australia Post is justifiably proud of its stamps – colourful and beautifully printed, they are a collector's dream. You can buy first-day covers and all sorts of special packages at any post office.

Other services include mail-holding, Poste Restante and redirection of mail. All GPOs have Post Restante counters, a free service which will hold mail for you for one month if you have no address of your own. Make sure the name and surname are printed clearly. To collect mail you need identification, and if you are collecting on behalf of another person you need both that person's ID and a signed letter authorizing you to do so. If you are changing address, you can arrange redirection of mail. Go to your local post office, fill out a form, pay $3.50, and make sure you have identification (and your new address!) with you. This service lasts a month and can be renewed – with payment of another fee – as you wish.


## ★ Motor Vehicles: Hiring, Buying, Insuring ★

For every 1000 people in Australia, there are over 500 motor vehicles. Most families have at least one car and it is the normal means of transport for work, business and leisure for millions of Australians.

While you can usually commute to work by public transport, as long as you work the standard rat-race hours, you may find yourself lost at weekends when your friends are whizzing off for a couple of days down the country. And with the suburbanization of shopping centres, you will miss out on the best value and choice if you have to shop in the city centre for lack of transport.

One good point about driving is that petrol costs about 60c a litre. But with the distances involved, it would want to.

Lots of people buy a car immediately on arrival in Australia, hardly stopping to unpack first. Others spend a year there without buying one. The choice really depends on your own situation. Migrants arriving in the city where they intend to settle are going to need one sooner or later, and may as well buy it sooner. If they do not have work lined up, it will help to be able to work anywhere within a reasonable distance – something not always possible using public transport.

On the other hand, working holidaymakers will find that they can pay for quite a few hire cars and taxis with the price of buying and running a car. One extra point to consider, for those arriving in Perth and intending to travel around, is that it is a very, very long way to anywhere. If you buy a car there, it must be in pretty good condition if you want to bring it east.

## CAR HIRE

Hiring a car can be a way of getting a weekend away from the city, or of breaking away from the main public transport routes when you are on holiday. With a group of you sharing, it can work out pretty cheap. The three major national car hire companies are Avis, Hertz and Budget. Then there are a host of smaller companies that operate only in one city, town or even from only one garage.

There is strong competition in the car hire business, so look out for special deals. Try a couple of places and ask each of them for a deal or a cut. Anything more than two days should qualify for some discount off the standard daily rate – ask about weekend, weekly or four-day rentals.

The big companies offer newer cars, greater choice and special features like one-way rentals (driving a car from one city to another) and airport pick-ups. Their lowest rates range upwards from $50 a day. The opposition, the smaller companies, will usually have older cars, but you can normally get a car from them for about $35 a day, basic.

There are lots of things to take into account when picking a company and striking a bargain. You must usually choose between a city rental (with unlimited kilometres) and a country rental (where you pay from 18 cents a kilometre and may or may not get the first couple of hundred free). Insurance may or may not be included in the quoted price; usually it is not. As well as the standard insurance, you can

100

pay extra for insurance to cover your liability for the first several hundred dollars of any claim; this is known as a collision damage waiver. Check too whether there are any special restrictions on where you can use the car. Some companies hire little two-cylinder Handyvans, but will not let you take them outside the town. In other areas, like far north Queensland, the Northern Territory and northern WA, you will probably want to use gravel roads. Most hire contracts have a woolly clause about using the car on 'unmade' roads. Find out exactly what they mean.

Car hire companies prefer credit cards to cash, but most will take cash too. When you have chosen a company, bring in your licence(s) and sign a credit card charge docket which is put away until you return. Ask about the rules for petrol (usually full tank out, full tank back) and away you go. You may of course tear off up goat tracks, ford rivers and go bush in your hired car, but going outside your area of use may void your insurance and you will be in deep trouble if you break down or crash while driving somewhere you were not supposed to be in the first place.

## MOKES

These are little, semi-open tin boxes on wheels that are often cheaper to hire than cars. They are great fun in a warm place and well worth hiring for a day, just for fun. Remember, though, that they only *look* like four-wheel drives, and are not meant for off-road driving. They give you very little protection in a crash and there is really no place to lock your valuables in a Moke.

## MOTORCYCLES

These are very popular in Australia, and one can understand why when the main drawback, the rain, is missing for much of the year. But all the other disadvantages are there – bike-blind drivers in cars and trucks, potential vandalism and a high rate of death and injury among bike riders. If you are considering touring, go for a good big four-stroke. The distances are just too great for smaller machines.

## BUYING A CAR

This transaction carries the same pitfalls in Australia as anywhere, with a couple of extra ones. You have three ways to go: private sales, dealers and auctions. This is, of course, for second-hand cars. If you have the money for a new car, you will get lots of advice for free from the car salesmen.

Private sales and auctions will be cheaper for any given year and model, but it is that much harder to check the car out thoroughly if it is in an auction yard and you are allowed to do no more than look at it. Private sellers are not obliged to give you any sort of guarantee.

Used-car salesmen (they refer to the cars as 'pre-owned') are the same the world over – they would sell their grannies to turn a quid. Do not take their word for anything. On the other hand, dealers are covered by the local guarantee system and with a registered dealer you can be sure of the title of the car. That is, you can be sure he owns the car he is selling you. You can run into big problems if the car you buy in a private sale turns out to have thousands owing on it to a hire purchase company. Unfortunately, there is no easy way to establish that the private individual selling a car actually owns it.

Prices vary, but you can get mobile for under $1000. It is only recently that the bargain-hunter's ideal of the $500 car that just goes and goes faded away. Anything under $1000 is going to be an ancient heap. Many such cars date from the early 1970s and have the big, thirsty, six-cylinder engines that were standard in Australia at the time. Even with the low price of petrol, they can be costly on long trips. On the other hand, you may be lucky.

For $2000 you should get a more recent model, perhaps only ten years old, with some sort of guarantee; $3000 should buy you a reasonable car. If the dealer tries to pooh-pooh the statutory warranty and give you a forte warranty, do not be taken in. The forte warranty makes very expensive demands on the owner about servicing and maintenance in order to have any validity at all.

Stamp duty is payable on the sale of second-hand cars and is related to their price. Therefore, many buyers and sellers prepare a second receipt which understates the price (within reason). The practice is illegal, but widespread.

Time was when you were crazy to buy anything but a Holden car if you intended going outside the cities in Australia. It was far easier to get spares for them. This is becoming less and less true. Chances are now that you will be able to get parts for established Japanese models like the Toyota Corolla quite easily. However, the Holden parts may be available on an abandoned car or from a breaking yard at a lower price than the new Japanese spare.

## THE GUARANTEE SYSTEM

This system varies from State to State and depends on the price of the car. In WA, for example, where the most basic guarantee comes in at $1500, you see an awful lot of cars on sale for $1499. Check the terms of the guarantee system in the State where you intend to buy. The best source of advice on things vehicular is the State motoring organization. Join as soon as you are sure you want to buy a car.

## REGISTRATION AND INSURANCE

In Australia, the legally required basic third party personal injury insurance is included with the registration – the equivalent of road tax here. Registration costs vary from State to State, and are governed by the age and size of the car, but it is worth buying a car with some months left to run on its registration. To register a new car, or renew it after the 12-month period is up, you must take it, in most States, to a licensed vehicle-testing station – many garages provide this service. They check it and (hopefully) issue a certificate of roadworthiness. Other States allow renewal of registration without requiring the mechanical check each time. The advantages of buying an already registered car are obvious: if your bargain crock fails the MOT equivalent and doesn't get its roadworthiness certificate, you can forget about it. Some States make more stringent mechanical demands than others.

The certificate of roadworthiness must then be taken to a motor registry office, where you pay the registration fee and third party insurance premium. They issue a windscreen sticker giving month and year of registration and the date of expiry.

It is worth knowing that you can apply to the Department of Motor Transport in each State for a printout of your car's registration form. This contains the names and addresses of previous owners as well as the details of chassis, licence and engine numbers. Where there is confusion or suspicion that the car may not be owned by the person selling it, and he or she has failed to provide any other proof, such as a bill of sale or a release from a hire purchase company, this could be useful.

When you move to another State to live, you have to get a new licence (number) plate, and change to that State's registration system.

Even though registration covers your legal need for insurance, it is worth paying at least for third party damage cover. You can run up quite a bill by writing off someone else's brand-new car in a collision. Some British insurance companies have reciprocal arrangements or affiliations with Australian counterparts and it may be possible, with a little persuasion, to transfer no claims bonuses. It is worth shopping around for the best deal. As well as your policy, get a letter from the old company stating the amount of your no claims bonus. Failing transfer arrangements, a refund should be obtainable from the old company for the unused portion of the policy.

STATE MOTORING ORGANIZATIONS

The motoring organizations are:

● National Roads and Motorists Association (NSW and ACT);
● Automobile Association of the Northern Territory;

- Royal Automobile Club of Queensland;
- Royal Automobile Association of South Australia;
- Royal Automobile Club of Western Australia;
- Royal Automobile Club of Tasmania;
- Royal Automobile Club of Victoria.

The majority of Australians belong to one or other of these organizations; their services are seen as practical, rather than an expensive luxury. For an annual fee of about $40 they will provide towing, insurance opportunities, advice and mechanical inspections. Membership in one State suffices, as they are all affiliated. They have reciprocal arrangements with the AA or RAC in Britain, so bring your UK membership card. If you are staying a long time, an official transfer of membership will be necessary; you can get a credit on the unused portion of your UK membership. Your organization will detail the guarantee scheme in your State and most publish a leaflet on buying a used car. See Chapter 12 for addresses.

Unless you are mechanically expert, it is worth the $50 or so that the motoring organizations charge to give a thorough check to the car you are thinking of buying. If the seller will not allow you to have it inspected, be suspicious, particularly when you are talking about an expensive (over $5000) car.

The organizations will also tell you the legal requirements for buying a car. In NSW, for example, each car can only be sold with a pink slip certifying its roadworthiness. If the owner has already got one, so much the better. In WA, on the other hand, the car need only be inspected if the registration has been allowed to lapse and you want to renew it, so buy a car that is still registered. Re-registering a car from another State can be a hassle, so buy one registered in the State you are in.


OUTBACK DRIVING

There are problems to look out for if you are going to drive in the outback. It is only in the 1980s that sealed (surfaced) roads were completed right around Australia and from Darwin down to Adelaide. Many of the smaller roads are extremely rough. For long trips in remote areas, stick to the sealed highway.

Take elementary precautions before heading off. Pack basic spares (fanbelt, spare oil, etc.) and the tools to fit them. Make sure your car is sound, not forgetting the tyres and the spare. If you are not using one of the main highways, ensure that the one you want to use is suitable for your vehicle and that there is plenty of petrol available along it. Carry plenty of water. You can collapse from dehydration very quickly in the inland desert in summer. Many people also carry a second spare tyre and a temporary windscreen, if travelling in remote areas.

## ON THE ROAD

Distances in Australia are enormous, so plan for stop-overs. Beware of fatigue, too. One stretch of the Perth–Adelaide highway runs over 140 km without a bend of any sort. It can be mesmerizing and sleep-making, but gum trees are very unyielding things to hit at speed.

Almost as unyielding are the animals. A kangaroo can weigh enough to write off your car if you hit one. You will notice a lot of Australian cars have 'roo-bars' on the front to fend them off, but even these do not offer complete protection as the animal can come through the windscreen or the impact with the bar can twist the chassis of the car. The answer adopted by most Australians is to drive only in daylight hours in roo-full areas. Watch out too for cattle, buffaloes, wild horses and donkeys, camels and wombats.

On a long trip, look out for the signs telling you where your next petrol is. It is no fun at all to hitch a hundred miles to fetch petrol after you run out. Last, but not least, among the dangers are road trains. These are articulated lorries of up to four trailers and up to 50 metres in length. Give them plenty of space and do not underestimate the amount of space you need to pass one. Look out too for the yards where the road trains are put together (they are not allowed into cities without being broken up).

# 8

# DUNNIES, DINGOES AND DINKY DIS
## The Language

One explanation for the Australian accent is that it comes of having to keep the lips close together to keep the flies out. Whatever you think about that theory, there are certainly enough colourful words and expressions to make you wonder sometimes whether English and Australian are one and the same language. Here is a short introduction to the wonderful world of strine – Australia's own language. Words of Aboriginal origin are marked (A).

| | |
|---|---|
| Abo | Aboriginal: offensive, but common. |
| Amber fluid | beer. |
| Arvo | afternoon. |
| Award | salary, rate of pay. |
| Back of Bourke | far away, remote. |
| Bail up | hold up, rob. |
| Banana bender | Queenslander. |
| Barbie | barbecue. |
| Barramundi (A) | the giant perch, *Lates calcarifer*, great sport and very good to eat. |
| Bathers | swimming togs. |
| Battler | a fighter, someone who has to struggle to get by. |

| | |
|---|---|
| Beaut! | that's good! |
| Bewdie | like beaut. |
| Bikie | motorcyclist. |
| Blowie or blowfly | bluebottle. |
| Bludger | scrounger, as in dole-bludger. |
| Blue | a row. |
| Bond | deposit. |
| Boomerang (A) | curved throwing weapon, as recorded by early settlers. |
| Bonzer | good. |
| Boong | Aboriginal: offensive, but common. |
| Bottle shop | off-licence. |
| Brumby (A) | wild horse. |
| Bush | country, as in 'go bush' and 'bushed' (lost). |
| BYO | Bring Your Own, a restaurant to which you bring your own wine or beer. |
| Chiko roll | revolting type of fast food. |
| Chook | chicken. |
| Chunder | vomit. |
| Cockie | small farmer, also cockatoo. |
| Cooee | what you call when you're bushed. |
| Compo | compensation. |
| Cozzy | swimming gear, from costume. |
| Crim | criminal. |
| Crook | unwell, equally for people, animals and cars. |
| Currawong (A) | a large black bird, *Strepera graculina*. |
| Cut-lunch | sandwiches. |
| Dag, daggy | dirt that clings to a sheep's rear, also a term of abuse. |
| Damper | flour and water mix, cooked on a stick in a fire in the bush. |
| Dill | fool. |
| Dilly, Dillybag (A) | formerly a native woven bag, extended to mean European-style bags. |
| Dingo (A) | a wild dog, and a term of abuse for people. |
| Dinky di | a 'real' Australian. |
| Dob in | to inform on. |

| | |
|---|---|
| Double dip | to cheat, as in claiming dole and working. |
| Drongo | useless person. |
| Duna | duvet. |
| Dunny | toilet. |
| Durex | one to watch . . . adhesive tape. |
| Fair dinkum | true, straight up. |
| Fair go | an appeal to someone's sense of fair play. |
| Financial | in the money. |
| Flake | shark meat. |
| Floater | fast food, consisting of a meat pie floating in pea soup, topped with tomato ketchup. |
| Fossick | prospect for gold or gems, to potter around. |
| Galah | silly person, from pink bird. |
| Garbo | a bin-man; and, similarly, postie, milko. |
| G'day | hello – yes, they really say it. |
| Give it away | give it up, quit. |
| God botherer | religious person, especially missionary or charismatic. |
| Good on yer | well done. |
| Grazier | big farmer. |
| Grog | drink. |
| Hoon | rogue, lair. |
| Humpy | Aboriginal shelter. |
| Interstate | every state except the one you are in. |
| Jackaroo | cowboy; female equivalent is a Jillaroo. |
| Joey | young kangaroo. |
| Journo | you guessed it, a journalist. |
| Koala (A) | tree-dwelling marsupial with a far better public image than it deserves. |
| Kookaburra (A) | large kingfisher, *Dacelo gigas*, famous for its lovely call that sounds like a laugh. |
| Lamington | small, square cake, invented in Australia. |
| Lair | layabout, ruffian. |
| Larrikin | a rogue. |
| Layby | to put a deposit on something in a shop. |
| Lollies | sweets; and lolly-water, lemonade. |
| Lurk | a plan or racket, often entertained by a 'lurk merchant'. |

| | |
|---|---|
| Mallee (A) | eucalypt shrub; also a district. |
| Manchester | linen and sheet department in a store. |
| Mate | friend, on the one hand one of the most valued institutions of Australian male life, mateship; other people just use it like a full stop, to end every sentence. |
| Mick | a Catholic. |
| Mozzie | mosquito. |
| Never never | real outback, back of Bourke. |
| New Australian | recent immigrant. |
| No worries | that's OK, that's right. |
| Ocker | crude Australian stereotype: offensive. |
| Off-sider | helper, assistant. |
| OS | overseas, as in 'he met her OS'. |
| Pademelon (A) | small wallaby (which, in turn, is a small macropod or kangaroo-like animal). |
| Pastoralist | large farmer. |
| Polly | politician. |
| Pom | British person, often in the phrase 'whingeing Pom'. |
| Push | group of larrikins, a gang. |
| Rage | social event |
| Ramp, rort | scheme, racket, sharp practice. |
| Ratbag | untrustworthy. |
| Ratshit | not very good. |
| Retrench | to make redundant, to lay off. |
| Ripper | great, fantastic. |
| Road train | multi-section juggernaut. |
| Root | to copulate. If you say harmless things like 'rooting in a drawer' dinki di Aussies will fall around laughing. |
| Schooner | large beer glass; there are also ponies, pots, butchers and middies. |
| Sea wasp | the deadly box-jellyfish. |
| Sealed road | surfaced road. |
| See you later | means goodbye, with no necessary intention of ever seeing someone again. |
| Shit-hot | good. |
| Shithouse | bad. |

| | |
|---|---|
| Shoot through | leave in a hurry. |
| Sickie | sick leave from work. |
| Smoko | short break from work. |
| Squatter | large land-owning farmer. |
| Stickybeak | nosey person; 'have a stickybeak' means to have a snoop. |
| Stubby | small bottle of beer. |
| Stuffed | of a person in bad way, tired; of an object, broken. |
| Sunbake | sunbathe. |
| Surfies | surfing fanatics. |
| Taipan (A) | the very venomous snake, *Oxyranus scutellatus*. |
| Tall poppies | achievers, targets for begrudgers. |
| Technicolour yawn | vomit. |
| Tinny | can of beer. |
| Thongs | flip-flops, universal Aussie summerwear. |
| Tucker | food. |
| Two-up | mad Australian gambling game, as seen in *Crocodile Dundee*. |
| True blue | genuine Australian. |
| Up himself | superior, snobbish. |
| Ute | Utility, or open-backed truck. |
| Walkabout | to give away responsibilities and wander off, to disappear. |
| Wet, the | monsoon season up north. |
| Wharfie | docker. |
| Whinge | to moan, to complain. |
| Wog | anyone to whom English is a second language. |
| Wowser | a spoilsport, a prude. |
| Yabby (A) | delicious freshwater, prawn-like fish. |
| Yakka (A) | work, as in 'hard yakka'. |
| Youi (A) | yes. |
| Your shout | your round. |

# 9

# WHAT'S WHERE
## Cities and States

## ★ Sydney ★

The establishment of a penal colony at Sydney Cove in 1788 is seen as the beginning of modern Australia. This is the event that was celebrated in 1988 with the country's bicentennial. Sydney is Australia's largest and oldest city, with a population of almost 3.5 million and a sprawling metropolis around a busy modern heart. Perhaps its most striking aspect is the amount of high-rise buildings in the central business district. With the lifting of height restrictions in 1957 Sydney just shot upwards. Highest of these is Centre Point Tower, open to the public – for a fee; the view from the top gives a very good orientation to the city. You can see the harbour, beaches and endless undulating suburbs, with the Blue Mountains in the distance, the features for which Sydney is loved. Sydney's best-known landmarks are the Opera House and the Harbour Bridge.

Built in 1932, the Harbour Bridge provides the main traffic artery from the northern suburbs to the city centre, and is crossed by an enormous number of cars each day. A pylon can be climbed if you are prepared to brave the traffic fumes and pay 50 cents. You can walk across it for nothing. The view of the harbour – though slightly obscured by an anti-suicide fence – is worth the effort.

Ferries are another of Sydney's major attractions. They leave from Circular Quay and a trip to the suburb of Manley or Taronga

Park Zoo – if you cannot afford actually to live on the harbour and commute by ferry every day – should not be missed.

Sydney has a number of old buildings which have been beautifully restored. The main shopping street is George Street, the most interesting feature of which is the Queen Victoria Building, a lavishly restored market building which now houses expensive shops and restaurants. Nearby is the Town Hall, which has a huge organ, with pipes covering one whole wall.

As well as Hyde Park, a rather over-used square in the city centre, notable only for the wild possums which inhabit its trees and frighten unsuspecting lovers on park benches, Sydney has the Domain and Botanical Gardens, a huge area beside the Opera House which is a very pleasant escape from the busy, noisy, rather dirty city centre.

Kings Cross is the sleazy area, full of sex shops and cheap accommodation. A handy place to live if you are in Sydney for a short while, it contains much of the city's nightlife. Oxford Street, leading to Paddington and the eastern suburbs, is another rather rundown street of restaurants, shops and pubs (many gay).

Bondi has to be Sydney's most famous suburb. The beach is small and rather scruffy, but here you may see the surfers and beach culture – golden, tanned people, keep-fit fanatics, surf life-saving clubs going through daring manoeuvres, watched by busloads of Japanese tourists.

There is a lot to see and do in Sydney and most tourists will visit it at some stage, if only because they feel it has to be done. As a city to live in, it has tremendous potential for career and social opportunities, with of course the attendant problems (mostly of street crime, pollution and godforsaken suburbs) apparent in any large urban mass. For those who crave the bright lights and excitement in Australia, Sydney is the place to be.

## ★ New South Wales ★

This is the most populous, most industrialized and most highly urbanized of the States. With a population of about 5.5 million it covers an area of 801,600 km$^2$ or 10.4% of the total area of Australia. It provides 36% of all goods manufactured in the country and 24% of Australia's mining products. As well as Sydney there are two other large industrial centres, Newcastle and Wollongong. Eighty kilometres south of Sydney, Wollongong has a population of over 236,000 and became notorious during 1987 for an outbreak of Legionnaires' Disease.

The countryside in New South Wales ranges from rich agricultural land, through plains and sheep country, to dusty outback. The coastal region provides sheltered resorts and dramatic scenery: Byron Bay and Coffs Harbour are two especially popular spots. As with much in Australia, the State's size means variety is the name of the game. The Hunter Valley is the centre of the wine industry. Griffith, a major agricultural and market gardening centre, has a large Italian population and was at one time the hub of a thriving marijuana industry. In the north-west of New South Wales, towards the Queensland border, is an area of dry plains and dust, the centre of which, Bourke (800 km NW of Sydney), is a byword for the real outback.

Broken Hill, a mining town 1170 km west of Sydney, provides an oasis of interest in a bleak landscape. This, the far west of New South Wales, is also dry, dusty country, but it contains remnants of mining days and Aboriginal settlements.

The area south-west of Sydney, moving towards Melbourne, is mostly pastoral and agricultural. Goulburn and Albury are the major population centres of this quiet farming country. The Murray River forms much of the boundary between NSW and Victoria.

The Murray River and its tributaries, the Darling, Murrumbidgee, Lachlan, Goulburn and many small rivers, has a catchment area which extends not only over much of New South Wales but also over a large part of southern Queensland and much of Victoria. It is the largest river system in Australia. About 80% of the country's irrigated land is within this river system and 60% of the exploitable surface water is used. All around the system are areas of fruit, vegetable and grape production.

# ★ Melbourne ★

Founded in 1835, Melbourne has been vying with Sydney ever since. Of similar size, with a population of over 2.9 million, it is always considered to be Australia's second most important city. For years it was the main centre for banking and finance in Australia, though its importance in this area is diminishing. Very different from Sydney, it is a city of substantial, grey buildings and wide, straight streets. It is often compared with a city in Europe, especially Paris, and its weather is the subject of many jokes. It does rain a lot in Melbourne, though many say it is a friendlier, more lively city in which to live than any of the others. There is a substantial Greek population and many Asians, especially Vietnamese, have settled there.

Of particular interest is its National Gallery, acknowledged to have the greatest collection of Australian Romantic paintings. Historic buildings include the Royal Mint and St James Cathedral (1872 and 1842 respectively) beside Flagstaff Gardens, and the Old Melbourne Gaol, now a penal museum. It contains death masks of famous bushrangers and convicts, and Ned Kelly's armour. The Victoria Market is excellent for cheap fruit and vegetables; on Sundays it becomes a general market. It is on the corner of Peel and Victoria Streets in North Melbourne.

The tram system in Melbourne is the main source of public transport. Attractive, old-fashioned and jolting, a ride in one is not to be missed – most typically at rush hour when they are crammed impossibly full of sweating humanity. They are symbols of Melbourne in the way the Opera House is of Sydney. The most interesting suburbs of Melbourne are Carlton, inner-city and new-fashionable; Toorak, the most exclusive area, and headquarters of the 'old money' for which Melbourne is famous; and St Kilda, the seaside suburb and sin centre. The city is the centre of Australia's motor vehicle industry and an important manufacturing centre. The port of Melbourne is the country's busiest general cargo port, though not the largest – Sydney has that distinction.

# ★ Victoria ★

Known as the 'Garden State', Victoria, with its area of rich soil and grasslands, particularly around the Murray River System, produces 20% of Australia's total agricultural and pastoral output. Robinvale and Mildura (550 km from Melbourne), north towards the New South Wales border, are major centres for the growth of grapes and citrus fruit. Further to the north-west is the Mallee region, an area of unproductive, dry bushland and sparse population which gets even emptier and bleaker as you move towards Broken Hill in NSW. The rest of the countryside around the Murray River would be similar to this, were it not for the major irrigation schemes started in the latter part of the nineteenth century.

To the west of Melbourne is the rich sheep and pastoral country of the Western District, stretching as far as the South Australian border. Hamilton is the centre of this area, which was the cause of explorer Thomas Mitchell describing the country as 'Australia Felix' – the lucky country.

The Mornington Peninsula and Phillip Island, south-east of Melbourne, are popular resort areas with good beaches. Further along the south coast is Wilson's Promontory, containing a National Park. The western coastline is more spectacular and rugged, with pretty coastal towns which were once centres of the whaling industry.

Another industrial city in Victoria is Geelong – population 130,000, south-west of Melbourne. Victoria is not all attractive countryside: it is an important manufacturing State, holding one-third of Australia's total means of industrial production, based mostly in Melbourne, Geelong, and the Latrobe Valley.

# ★ Adelaide ★

The population of Adelaide is under one million. Estimated in 1984 to be 978,900, this comparatively small number is reflected in the quietness of the city's streets and the relaxed, almost provincial atmosphere of the city centre. Adelaide is a beautiful sunny city, on the banks of the Torrens River, flanked by the hills of the Mount Lofty ranges. It used to be known as 'the city of churches' and it does have many attractive old churches. It also has a modern Festival Centre, located on the south bank of the Torrens, where Australia's premier Arts Festival is held every second year – 1990 is one of those years, and it will take place over three weeks in late February and early March, with guest performers and speakers from all over the world participating in dance, drama, music, art and workshop events. Adelaide is a well-planned city, with wide streets of imposing stone buildings. The effect is similar to Melbourne, but somehow lighter and cleaner, perhaps because the stone used is paler in colour.

North Adelaide is one of the most fashionable suburbs, full of restored bluestone houses; Melbourne Street is its exclusive shopping street. The seaside suburb of Glenelg can be reached on Adelaide's only tramline, which departs from Victoria Square. Not to be missed is the long, winding drive up to the peak of Mount Lofty. This takes you through the hill suburbs, devastated in the 1983 bushfires. You need a car – or bicycle if you are super-fit – but the view of the whole city, suburbs and sea stretched out below you is worth the effort.

Adelaide is a very pleasant city in which to live, with its attractive layout and buildings, a green belt of parkland around the city, and nearby hills and wineries to which you can escape from the rigours of work. Perhaps rather peaceful for some tastes, but the presence of two universities (Flinders and Adelaide) should provide more than enough young people to ensure a lively social scene.


## AUSTRALIAN FORMULA ONE GRAND PRIX

The first Grand Prix took place here in 1985 and was such a success it has been repeated annually in late October or early November. For five days the town is taken over by the world of motor racing and food and accommodation become scarce and expensive. The race is actually run through the city's streets and is a must for anyone interested in this sport.

117

# ★ South Australia ★

This State was established as a colony by a private company in 1836. It differs from the other States in that it was never a penal settlement, with the free convict labour for public building that that system entailed. Instead, the nurture of private enterprise and personal industriousness has left its mark on the many small-scale farms and wineries, carefully planted trees and well-kept, tamed countryside evident in many parts of South Australia.

From the early days, this State came under German influence, beginning with Lutherans settling there in 1839 to escape religious persecution in Europe. Hahndorf, a town 29 km south-east of Adelaide, is very Germanic, and worth a visit although it is very touristy.

The resident population of South Australia is around 1,358,000. Most live in Adelaide or the other industrial centres. Elizabeth is a satellite town of Adelaide, a centre of the motor manufacturing industry. Whyalla, on the west coast of the Eyre Peninsula, is an important steel-producing centre and deep-water port. Port Augusta, at the head of the Spencer Gulf, is a crossroads for goods and people going in all directions and an electricity generating centre.

The more densely populated agricultural areas are around the Murray River System, the centre of which is Renmark, 295 km from Adelaide. South Australia is best known for its wine production. If you enjoy visiting wineries the Barossa Valley (50 km south-east of Adelaide) will be of interest. The major town in the south-east is Mount Gambier (population 20,000).

South Australia has always been a very agricultural State, though this is changing, with primary production now employing only 7% of the workforce. Of the gross value of Australia's agricultural production this State contributes 13% in crops, 11% in livestock products and 9% in livestock slaughterings. Major agricultural products are wheat, barley, wine, beef, lamb and wool. Interestingly, it is also the driest State. Its arid climate means only 10% of the land is usable for cropping or permanent pasture.

As you move further north, you get into extremely desolate country of searing heat and dry salt lakes. The route towards Alice Springs from Adelaide is worth travelling, especially if you can pass through Coober Pedy, an opal-mining town which is mostly built underground to escape the heat.

To the far west of the State is fairly flat grain country, eventually becoming the expanse of the Nullarbor Desert, the huge land barrier between South Australia and Western Australia.

## ★ Hobart ★

This is the second oldest, the smallest and the southernmost State capital. Originally founded at Risdon Cove in 1803, the colony was moved about 10 km down the river the following year. There it, or at least its centre, remains on the Derwent River, under the shadow of 1270-metre Mount Wellington.

Today it is a bustling city of 180,000 people. Those who feel a longing for British weather should consider a visit. It rains an average of 162 days a year, more than any other State capital, and it rarely gets hot in summer. In winter, it gets quite cold.

Much of the old town centre, far more than in most Australian cities, remains intact. The presence of convict (for which read 'unpaid' or even 'slave') labour in its early days meant that substantial public, commercial and private buildings were possible. The activity of the town centred on the port in its early days, as fortunes were made in whaling, ship-building and in exporting the rich produce of Tasmania. From this time the buildings of Salamanca Place and Battery Point, down by the harbour, remain.

It is also worth visiting the Cadbury's factory, which must have one of the most beautiful factory sites in the world, on a bend in the Derwent. Regrettably they charge an admission fee ($5 in early 1987). Other points of interest are the Tasmanian Museum and Art Gallery, in Hobart's oldest building, the Commissariat Store built in 1808, and the 1811 Anglesea Barracks. The barracks is still used by the army, but is open to the public, free of charge, on weekdays.

119

# ★ Tasmania ★

Over 40% of Tasmanians live in and around Hobart, which leaves the rest of the island's 68,000 km$^2$ relatively lightly populated. Indeed, much of the west coast, particularly the south-western end, is wilderness, with no settlements of any size.

Tasmania's major products are woodchip, paper and wood products, foodstuffs – and chocolate! Fishing and tourism are also important income earners. Because of its natural abundance of suitable sites for hydro-electric generation, Tasmania also sells electricity.

Probably Tasmania's biggest attraction for tourists is its wilderness. The most famous bushwalk in Australia, the Cradle Mountain–Lake St Clair Overland Track is mentioned in Chapter 10 under Seven Things Not to Miss, but there are many other areas to be explored on foot. Maria Island, off the east coast, is a peaceful wildlife sanctuary in which you can see wallabies, kangaroos and Cape Barron geese at close range.

The central west coast bears the scars of the attitude that has been all too common in the white man's dealings with Australia – dig it up, chop it down and flog it. There are a whole range of mines and mining towns, some still producing, others deserted. The hills around the town of Queenstown have been turned into a moonscape of bare rock by mining.

Also on the west coast is the port of Strahan, the base for cruises up the beautiful Gordon River. When the river is high enough, the cruises go right up to the junction with the Franklin River, where the State government intended flooding thousands of acres of virgin forest to generate yet more electricity. The plan was abandoned after pressure from the Federal government and a world-wide outcry. David Bellamy, the British naturalist, played a major role.

In the south-eastern corner of Tasmania is the Tasman Peninsula, with the remains of the convict settlement at Port Arthur. It was with great glee the British discovered that the peninsula was a natural prison, and in 1830 it was chosen as a place to confine prisoners who had committed crimes in the colony. The neck of the peninsula is narrow enough for the authorities to have chained dogs at intervals across it to make escape impossible.

Among the best-preserved buildings is the horrible Pentonville-style radial prison, designed to break the spirits of 'difficult' prisoners, or drive them mad by sensory deprivation.

Tasmania is well set up with campsites and hostels. There are a great many things to see and none of them is too far from the rest. These facts, and the friendliness of many local people, make up for the extra trouble and expense of getting there from the mainland.

# ★  Brisbane  ★

Situated in the south-eastern corner of Queensland, Brisbane is about 30 km inland from Moreton Bay. Of similar size to Perth, with a population of about one million, it is a more bustling city. This is possibly because of its role as a gateway to the heavily promoted tourists' paradise that is Queensland. Brisbane is the jumping-off point for the coastal resorts of the Gold Coast, Sunshine Coast and the Great Barrier Reef.

The city was established as a penal colony in 1824 and remained one until 1842. During that time no free men were allowed within 80 km of the city. It was eventually thrown open for free settlement after pressure from jealous would-be settlers who could see its potential – this spirit of entrepreneurship is still apparent in the business world of Brisbane today.

The city has an interesting mixture of old and new buildings and is given character by the gentle hills sloping up from the big loop in the Brisbane River upon which it is based. The City Hall (1930) is a huge building on Anne Street which houses the city's entire civic organization. The square immediately in front of it, King George Square, is in many ways the focal point of the central city area. Most important of Brisbane's public buildings is the Cultural Centre. Located in South Brisbane, on the banks of the river, it is a major new development containing the Museum, Art Gallery, auditoria and restaurants and a huge exhibition centre. It was built for the 1988 international exposition, World Expo 88.

There are short cruises and day trips available on the river. Koala fanciers would enjoy a trip to the Lone Pine Koala Sanctuary, one of the many places where you can cuddle the creatures. Even Pope John-Paul II held a koala on his visit to Australia in 1986.

Brisbane is not a major manufacturing centre, though it does have a busy port with trade in containers, bulk cement and sugar. It is a major convention centre, though, with many big hotels and conference facilities. Its capacity in this area was boosted in 1982, when it hosted the Commonwealth Games.

With a wide choice of restaurants and some very fashionable shops, Brisbane would be a good choice of city in which to live. It has plenty of sunshine – an average seven and a half hours of it a day – an interesting ethnic mix, a good location for holidays and weekends away, and is small enough to be friendly yet large enough to be a lively place. One drawback is that work – unless perhaps in the tourist trade – and reasonably priced long-term accommodation seem to be hard to come by.

# ★ Queensland ★

Second only to Western Australia in size, Queensland covers 22.5% of the continent and has a total area of 1,728,000 km². Otherwise totally unlike Western Australia, it has a sizeable population and a number of thriving regional centres and industrial towns as well as Brisbane. It is the third most populous State, with a population of over 2, 525,000 – 16% of the total population of Australia.

Agriculture, mining, manufacturing and tourism are all important industries. Queensland is a major source of income for Australia, producing 23% of the total value of the country's exports. If you also remember that Queensland is a favourite holiday destination for both native Australians and overseas tourists you may realize that it is a good source of casual work. Seasonal jobs, in agriculture or tourism, will be available somewhere in Queensland all year round. The difficulty, with such a huge State, may be in picking the right place at the right time.

## QUEENSLAND'S IMAGE

The State is cleverly marketed by a series of economic and tourism development agencies aided by an active State Government. As with New South Wales, Queensland is a State of infinite variety, with somewhere to suit all needs and tastes. It is also more exotic than the staider, colder, more southerly States. This is aided by its climate – more than half of the State lies within the tropics and this results in an excitingly different flora and fauna and agricultural produce. It is also seen as separate, somehow apart from the rest of Australia. People make Queensland jokes and call Queens-landers 'banana benders', but underlying this condescension is an almost envious regard for the State's differences.

## GEOGRAPHICAL OUTLINE

Geographically, the State of Queensland can be divided into four main sections. From the Gold Coast resort area on the New South Wales border to the outpost of Cooktown on the Cape York Peninsula in far North Queensland is the coastal strip, with almost endless beaches, many small islands and from Townsville onwards, the Great Barrier Reef. Surfer's Paradise, the centre of the Gold Coast, and Noosa, the centre of the Sunshine Coast, are Australia's answer to Benidorm and Torremolinos – all high-rise holiday apartments and amusement arcades. Perfect resorts if you enjoy that kind of place, they have one drawback. The high-rise apartments are so tall they sometimes cut the sun off the beaches in the early afternoon.

The further north you go along this coast the more deserted and tropical the beaches become. Crocodiles also become more frequent further north. Daintree (90 km north of Cairns, as far as you can go up this coast on a surfaced road) has a thriving tourist trade based on cruises to spot these unappealing reptiles.

There are a number of sizeable towns on the coastal strip, most of which are dependent on the tourist trade and used principally as departure points for islands and popular holiday spots along the coast. Important agricultural centres and also of interest to the tourist are: Maryborough (population 20,200, timber and sugar industries), Bundaberg (population 32,700, sugar, tobacco, fruit industries – and of course the knock-out, over-proof rum), Rockhampton (population 51,200, beef centre), and Mackay (population 35,600, sugar processing and export, coal export). Sugar is one of Queensland's major agricultural products. It is responsible for 95% of Australia's total production: everywhere one is surrounded by waving fields of sugar cane.

Inland from the coastal strip, the gentle slopes of the Great Dividing Range eventually give way to the rich agricultural tablelands region. Here, more sugar is grown, also peanuts, all kinds of tropical fruit, vegetables and grain. The Darling Downs is Australia's most fertile area of grain production, the centre of which is Toowoomba (population 64,000). As one moves further west and north, the vast plains of productive soil gradually give way to harsh countryside, flat and sparsely populated. This area is difficult to travel, with mostly unsurfaced roads and numerous dry riverbeds which flood periodically.

Mount Isa is the only major settlement in the outback, and it exists only because it is the site of one of the world's richest mines and the only one in the world where copper, silver, lead and zinc are found in quantity together. It is 887 km west of Townsville, with a population of 24,000.

## ★  Perth  ★

Perth is spacious and clean, with lots of parks. The wide stretches of the Swan River and other waterways around which it is built make it appear more like a purpose-built holiday resort than a city. The city centre itself is quite small, with a lot of soulless glass and concrete high-rise buildings. Very few of the city's old, quaint or historically significant buildings have survived the economic expansion of the last 25 years.

Sunny, with an excellent climate, Perth's major attractions are its parks and gardens, unpolluted beaches and the Swan River, all of which make for an outdoor, watersport-orientated existence. There are several wineries on the Swan River, about 25 km from Perth, and a cruise (from Barrack Street jetty, in the city centre) to one of these is an interesting if rather debauched experience. Among the beaches are Cottesloe, City Beach and Scarborough, each of which is nicer and cleaner than the world-famous Bondi in Sydney. The Swan River provides a venue for para-gliding, windsurfing and sailing, all very close to the city centre. Kings Park is a large tract of natural bushland and green parkland, also containing the Botanical Gardens, within walking distance of the city centre.

Perth's most interesting suburb is Fremantle, the original port for the city. It has the character and interesting old buildings, including many pubs, that the city centre lacks. Restored for the America's Cup in 1986, it is very much a young people's centre. There is a market there on Saturdays and Sundays.

The most exclusive suburb is Dalkeith, where the riverside mansions are the homes of many millionaires – of which Perth has a higher concentration than any other Australian city. The city is backed by the Darling Range of hills and is fringed by market gardens and soft-fruit farms. Rottnest Island, just off the coast, is a popular weekend destination. It is the only home of the quokka, a unique marsupial that looks like a cross between a rat and a squirrel.

Perth would be a clean, relaxed city in which to live, with tremendous potential for those who like outdoor sports. Its isolation and size do make it quiet and limited in terms of work opportunity and night life – especially in comparison with the major cities of the eastern States.

## PERTH'S ISOLATION

It is only in recent years that Perth has experienced major growth, largely as a result of exploiting Western Australia's mineral wealth. But it is still only the marketing and staging post for the rich fields of iron ore, nickel, oil and natural gas, many minerals and gold which are located in remote regions and off the coast in the far north and west of the State. Perth is not yet a major manufacturing centre – in 1984, in all of Western Australia there were only 4000 manufacturing establishments (employing 70,000 workers in total), and 80% of them were in the Perth area. Though this number has grown since then, mining-related work is still the city's biggest income earner.

The problem for Perth is the same now as when it was founded in 1829, and has to be considered in any discussion of the city. It is a very long way from anywhere else in Australia, with great areas of barren land and inhospitable desert forming a major transport and communications barrier, and it is the only major population centre in the State.

## ★ Western Australia ★

The massive state of Western Australia has an area of 2,525,500 km$^2$, almost one-third the total area of Australia. It is also very sparsely populated, with about 1,500,000 people – the majority of whom live in the south-west corner in Perth and a few other small population centres – making up only 8.8% of Australia's population. And it is a rich state, earning 23% of the national export income. Its mineral production is one-third of the total Australian output.

Much of the countryside is very barren, with two major desert areas, the Nullarbor Plain extending to the South Australian border in the south-west and the Great Sandy Desert lying between the mountainous gorge country of the Pilbara and Kimberley regions in the north. Between these two are also the Gibson Desert, extending to the Northern Territory border to the east, and the Great Victoria Desert, which runs as far as Coober Pedy in South Australia's far north.

The only real routes in Western Australia are right around the coast (there is a total 12,500 km of it), or the Eyre Highway which crosses the Nullarbor Plain to Adelaide, 2824 km away. Most of the agricultural land is in the south-west corner. Wheat and sheep are the major products and Northam (population 6800) and Narrogin (population 5000) are major towns of the wheatlands. Near Hyden, an unusual rock formation called Wave Rock is a popular tourist destination. See it if you are in the area – it doesn't really warrant the lengthy trip from Perth in its own right.

Below Perth, towards the south-west extremity of the State, is rolling golden pastoral country, the fruit-producing areas of Donnybrook and the wineries of Margaret River, followed by the coastal towns of Albany and Esperance. At least one shark attack occurred in the Esperance area in 1988, but these towns remain popular holiday spots for the people of Perth. Absolutely unforgettable in this area are the towering jarrah and karri forests, eucalypt varieties which are among the hardest and most durable of the world's woods. The centre for visiting these is the town of Pemberton. They are beautiful, tall, straight trees which grow up to 60 metres high. Some of the tallest were used until quite recently as lookout posts for bushfires, and you can climb one if you are feeling courageous.

North of Perth there is a lot of dry, flat bushland and some spectacular coastal scenery. Near Cervantes is the Pinnacles Desert. Further up the coast is Shark Bay, with the town of Denham (population 400) having the position of most westerly town in Australia. Twenty-six kilometres from Denham is Monkey Mia, where it is possible to play with schools of wild dolphins. Major places of interest further up this coast are few and very far between. The Pilbara region, with some impressive mountains and gorges, is an area of wild scenery. Broome is a pearling town with a developing tourist industry. Most of the other settlements in the far north are support towns for mining companies. The Kimberleys, the centre for which is Derby, is also an area of wild magnificence. Because distances are so vast in the north of Western Australia many people choose to fly between places of interest. About 600 km east of Perth, travelling towards Adelaide, are the old gold mining towns, Coolgardie and Kalgoorlie (population 20,000). Kalgoorlie is still a booming gold town.

## WESTERN AUSTRALIA'S WILDFLOWERS

In season (August to October) people travel from all over Australia to see the wildflowers of this State. Spectacular largely because of their quantity – they grow in profusion over vast areas – some are unique to the region. The most interesting, the Kangaroo Paw, is the symbol of Western Australia and popularly cultivated as a garden plant.

## ★ Darwin ★

On top of Australia's 'Top End', Darwin, capital of the Northern Territory, is a strange city. This is perhaps both because of its relative youth as a place of any importance, which really only stems from its position as first line of defence in the Second World War, and because of the kind of people who choose to live there.

Darwin's population numbers about 68,500 and they must all be the kind of people who enjoy climatic extremes and geographical isolation. City-wise, Darwin has the most of everything: most sunshine (an average of 8.5 hours a day), most rainfall (annual average 1536 millimetres), and highest mean temperatures for both the hottest and coldest months (hottest month 29.6°C, coldest month 25.1°C – hardly cool!). It is also well known for having the highest per-capita beer consumption in Australia.

Darwin is not only newly important, but also newly built. The resilience of the people who live there may be judged by the way they have twice rebuilt the city. It was almost completely destroyed by Japanese bombing raids during the Second World War and again by Cyclone Tracy in the early hours of Christmas morning 1974. The buildings of the new city are of undistinguished architecture and strangely scruffy – Darwin doesn't seem to have the careful planning of Canberra or the glossy office buildings of Perth or Brisbane. It does, however, have a character of its own and would be a fascinating city to visit or live in. It has a very transient workforce and is made more attractive by the tropical loading many pay awards contain. Casual work, especially fishing, labouring or in the tourist industry, appears to be relatively easy to come by.

Darwin's layout is made rather confusing by the site of its airport. Very close to the city centre, the suburbs have had to extend around it and most accommodation is a long way from the central city area. It is a good place in which to have a car, though public transport of a sort does exist.

## ★ Northern Territory ★

The Northern Territory is a vast area of 1,346,200 km$^2$, 17.5% of the Australian continent. Most of this is empty outback, with remote cattle stations, few settlements or surfaced roads. The main roads stretch away through red dusty countryside, and the wide-open spaces and harsh environment through which they pass is in many ways the classical concept of the real Australia.

Eighty per cent of the Northern Territory's area is in the tropics. The area around Darwin has two seasons, wet and dry. Everywhere is hot during the day, but the central desert area, around Alice Springs, gets very cold at night – often below freezing point in winter. The Northern Territory's chief industries are mining (mostly of uranium and bauxite), tourism, beef cattle production and agriculture. Agricultural production is quite limited, consisting mostly of cash crops grown on irrigated land in the Darwin area.

Tourism is rapidly developing and has replaced cattle as the Territory's second most important industry. The presence of Kakadu National Park and Ayers Rock within the Territory's borders help to make it a very popular destination. These features are dealt with in Chapter 10 under Seven Things Not to Miss, but there are also other places of interest within the State which deserve a visit. Unfortunately, its size and the locations of popular features make getting around a real problem. Darwin and Alice Springs may both be used as centres for visiting these areas – you can get buses between the two, and from them take organized trips to places of interest. Having your own car, though, especially in the Darwin–Katherine–Kakadu triangle and immediately around Alice Springs, is a definite advantage. Car hire in these areas would probably work out cheaper than taking a series of organized bus trips, with the exception of the 450 km journey to Ayers Rock.

There are few towns of any size in the Northern Territory other than Darwin. Alice Springs (1500 km south of Darwin) is the only other major centre. It has a population of over 24,000 and is important as a tourist base and supply centre for the settlements and stations of the outback. 'The Alice' disappoints many people – it is very modern, complete with shopping centres and a pedestrianized mall (Todd Street). Work in the tourist trade may be possible here – there is a large number of hotels and motels. Worth seeing are the Royal Flying Doctor Base, on Stuart Terrace, and the Old Telegraph Station (2 km north of the city centre).

Other towns of the Northern Territory are Katherine (population 4600) and Tennant Creek (population 2300). These are important as wayside stops for travellers on the Stuart Highway (the 'Track' which leads eventually to Adelaide) and as supply centres for the remote cattle stations of the outback. They are far closer to the image of a dusty outback town popularized in Nevil Shute's novel *A Town like Alice* than clean, modern Alice Springs itself.

## ★ Canberra and the Australian Capital Territory ★

With an area of 2359 km$^2$ and a population of about 265,000 the Australian Capital Territory is of interest to the tourist only as the site of the national capital. It is not the kind of place you would choose to settle in, and while it has pretty countryside and some nice bushwalks, there are other more spectacular places in Australia. Sixty per cent of all wage-earners living in Canberra are employed by government agencies or departments, so it is very much a civil service town.

Canberra is 320 km south-west of Sydney and 655 km north-west of Melbourne, centred around the man-made Lake Burley Griffin. This lake divides the city into two sections. One side of the lake is principally residential, the other (the south side) mostly devoted to business and administrative offices. This modern design makes for a very tidy, orderly city, with wide boulevards and rather inhuman proportions.

The scale of Canberra makes it daunting to walk around. Outside the city there are three independent satellite towns, Belconnen, Woden and Tuggeranong. Sixteen kilometres west of Canberra is the Australian National University's Stromlo Observatory. Containing a huge telescope and photographic exhibition, it is of interest to the astronomy buff. Tidbinbilla, 40 km north-west, has a space-tracking station, the Canberra Space Centre, which is also open to the public. There is a nature reserve nearby which has popular barbecue facilities and bushwalks.

The city is not exactly famous for its nightlife and closes almost entirely on public holidays. It did experience rapid growth, however, during the 1960s and early 1970s and as a result has a large young population. It is also the home of the Australian National University. These factors may make Canberra a more lively place in future, as it overcomes its artificial beginnings.

# 10

# GOING WALKABOUT
## Holidays and Travel

Australia is made for holidays. The traveller is well catered for and there are thousands of unique and beautiful things to see. If you are migrating, try to travel a bit before you get bogged down in work and other commitments. If that is impossible, fix a definite holiday time within your first six months. You will appreciate a break from the pressures of settling into a new life, and learn a lot about your adoptive country. It is possible to live for years in a city and never see a 'roo or a snake or get any idea of the vastness of the outback – all the things for which Australia is famous. A good plan for those on working holiday visas is to work for a longish period, save, travel, and spend it all, then repeat the process, working somewhere else. To stay in one place is definitely not the aim of a working holiday. Anyway, it is a shame to miss the experiences this country has to offer.

Tourism is Australia's biggest single industry and one of its fastest growth areas. In 1988 it contributed 6% of the gross domestic product and directly or indirectly provided over 430,000 jobs. In that year nearly 2 million tourists visited Australia and spent about $3,700 million. Figures have shot up since then, with intensive marketing campaigns at home and abroad, especially in Japan and America. Well-known figures such as Barry Humphries and Paul Hogan appear in television ads in Australia and overseas, and the States rival each other in their chauvinistic slogans. All Australians are exhorted to 'Smile and say G'day' to the money-spending tourists.

## ★ Types of Holiday ★

The problem with zipping from city to city, airport to airport and from one tourist magnet to another is missing all the bits in the middle. The strange experiences you have, the people you meet on the road, the glimpses of wild animals, the strange places you end up in and – most of all – the sense of covering distance, make travelling and holidaying in Australia unique. If you are short of time, it would be better to limit yourself to one area and travel overland rather than take an over-ambitious bunny-hopping round trip. It is less exhausting, cheaper and gives you a better feel for the true nature of the country. Use your judgement, though. Obviously, some parts are tiresome to travel through, while others have great variety. Tasmania's compactness and scenic variety, for example, are what make it a good holiday spot.

By far the best way to go in Australia is to camp. Having your own transport and accommodation and cooking for yourself make for a very cheap holiday. In addition, you are close to the natural world and get to see more wildlife than you ever would in a hotel or hostel. Wombats, possums, wallabies, bandicoots, emus and dingoes will come to visit, depending on where you are. Of course, camping in Australia in summer is far different from camping in Britain. Your worst enemy, the weather, is turned into your best friend.

The next best thing to camping is using youth hostels, which are numerous and well located in places of interest. If you are travelling in a group, on-site vans in caravan parks are also quite a good option. Holiday flats are useful, especially if you intend to live in a resort area for some time. Hotels and motels provide reasonable accommodation, but are expensive and rather limiting.

Australia is very much geared to adventurous outdoor holidays. Even in beach resorts, people spend more time snorkelling, wind-surfing and paragliding than they do lazing on the beach. Try bushwalking and outdoor pursuits and

133

visit as many National Parks as you can. They have excellent facilities, often free camp-grounds, information centres and ranger-guided walks. The whole idea is to get out of the cities and enjoy the wide-open spaces – they are Australia's best asset.

## ★ Information ★

There are three main sources of tourist information: guide books, tourist offices, and agencies such as the National Trust and the National Parks and Wildlife Service. A large number of guide books is available in Australia, from general guides to the whole country to those dealing with specialized interests such as wineries, wildflower areas or bushwalking. Try to limit yourself to one good general guide to take with you and use local tourist information. Research as much as you can before you take off on holiday – it is terrible to miss things out of ignorance of their existence. Some guide books are suggested in Chapter 13. Australians also love glossy photographic books and these are available for every area. Lovely to look at before you go, or to buy as a souvenir, they are too heavy and cumbersome to cart around.

Tourist information is free, for the most part. Before you leave Britain you can write to the Australian Tourist Commission, the organization which provides information for potential visitors. Its material is distributed overseas only and they have nothing to do with tourism within the country. Its London address may be found in Chapter 12.

Tourist promotion within Australia is handled by State government bureaux. They each have offices in most cities, a head office in the State capital, and numerous local offices in towns or places of interest. The local offices may have specialized information on the local area, unavailable elsewhere, so make a point of visiting them. State offices provide reservation services for transport, special tours and accommodation, as well as colourful guides and leaflets, good maps and quantities of information. They also have London offices.

The National Parks and Wildlife Service has information offices in each city and often in the National Parks themselves. Addresses for the city offices may be found in Chapter 12.

The National Trust is very similar to the British organization. Dedicated to preserving historic buildings, it provides information and walking-tour guides of main towns, usually free. Membership of the trust is a good idea if you are going to be in Australia for any length of time, as it gives you free entry to its properties, its magazine, and better access to information. Addresses of State offices may be found in Chapter 12.

## ★ How to Go ★

When deciding whether to fly, take a bus or train, or drive yourself, the most important factor must be your time – or lack of it. Most of us from a relatively small country totally underestimate the distances and time taken to travel in Australia – we are just not used to reading maps of that scale.

FLYING

The chief advantage of flying is its speed, particularly if you would otherwise be crawling over very boring terrain. You also have great comfort, aerial views and always some kind of snack – unless it is a terribly short flight. Alcoholic drink is usually extra on internal flights.

Flying is expensive, and there seems to be little true price competition. There are two major airlines, Ansett and Australian Airlines. East–West Airlines is a less expensive company, but it doesn't have the range of destinations of the big two. Cheapest ways to go are on Airpasses, covering a number of destinations, or Super Saver/Standby fares. Discounts are available for tourists who have recently arrived in the country and have an onward ticket. These are not well advertised, so ask.

The disadvantages of flying include the cost and hassle of

getting to and from airports, missing out on things at ground level, and, most of all, the price of the tickets.


## OVERLAND TRAVEL

The costs are surprisingly similar, whatever means you choose, when everything – fuel, food on the way, accommodation if you need it, books and magazines to kill the boredom, spares and emergency precautions if driving – is taken into consideration. The major exception is express bus travel, which is definitely the cheapest means of getting around.


## BUS TRAVEL

The best bet of all is to buy a ticket for your ultimate destination, rather than a pass or tickets for lots of intermediate short journeys. Most companies will allow you to break off and resume your journey without time limitations. The only difficulty here is timetable. Many express services travel through the night and may miss out on, or simply not stop at, intermediate points. You must also always reconfirm and reserve your onward journey, so allow a certain time flexibility – a bus with a spare seat may be harder to come by from Kalgoorlie than from a major city.

The major companies offer many different passes and discounts – including 10% less for those with International Student Identity Cards or Australian Youth Hostel Association (AYHA) Cards. Research prices carefully – and the limitations of time and timetable on inclusive passes – before buying. For example, a straightforward ticket from Perth to Sydney will allow you to stop at Adelaide, Melbourne and Canberra, and many other places in between, without time restrictions, whereas a pass (Koala Pass, Aussiepass etc.) provides unlimited kilometres within a certain period, at a far higher price. You've got to remember there's only so much ground you can cover in 15, 30 or 60 days – the danger with most bus passes is over-ambition.

Long-distance bus travel is surprisingly comfortable. It is

136

worth paying a bit extra for a comfortable coach: DeLuxe Bus Company's Superdeckers are particularly nice, with good reclining seats, video, cold drinking water, toilet and a great view from the top deck. If time isn't a problem, bus is the cheapest way to go.


TRAIN TRAVEL

There is nothing quite like a good long train trip. But trains in Australia are expensive. Tickets cost from 30% to 50% more than a bus would for the same journey. If you already own a car, taking a train or driving yourself would require similar amounts of money.

Trains are the slowest overland transport. Timetabling and frequency are also poor because of the great distances and small number of passengers on most express services. If you want to break your journey, your ticket will probably allow you to, but it can mean (as between Sydney and Brisbane) getting off the train and picking up the onward train in the middle of the night. Train travel has advantages, though, apart from the sheer joy of watching the countryside roll slowly by. You are likely to meet more Australians and fewer tourists than on buses. Because they get discounts, most of your fellow passengers will be railway workers or pensioners. The bar is a good place for making friends and whiling away the time with card games, chess and draughts.

The trains are comfortable, with a bar, dining carriage, showers and sleepers for most long journeys. Sleepers are expensive ($40–60 on top of your ticket), but the luxury is worth it if you can afford it. Most ordinary carriage seats are less comfortable for sitting or sleeping on than those on buses. Food and drink are a little more expensive than usual, but not exorbitant. Passes for unlimited distance within a set period are available, as for buses.

There are some really famous train journeys in Australia, and if you enjoy rail travel it is worth experiencing at least one long trip – perhaps the Ghan from Alice Springs to Adelaide, the Sunlander from Brisbane to Cairns, or the Indian Pacific right across the continent.

## CAR TRAVEL

The advantages of driving yourself are obvious – you are your own boss, can see everything, take your own time and detour as much as you like. Holidaying in your own car is in many ways the ideal way to go, but there are disadvantages. First, it is more expensive than the bus, especially as you are likely to be in a cheap second-hand car that drinks petrol. You will also find it slow and tiring. For most long journeys you will need at least two drivers in the car. Finally, the danger of driving at night, the precautions and spares you must take before going off into the outback, and the high prices charged for food and drink in most roadhouses mean that car travel is a holiday in itself as regards cost, rather than a means of getting from one place to another for your holiday to begin. If you own a car anyway, or can afford to hire one, driving is the most interesting way to go. For more information on the need for a car and the problems of hiring or buying one, see Chapter 7.

## ★ Seven Things Not to Miss ★

This is a short list of some things that make Australia a great holiday continent. Most are well-known tourist destinations and some, at least, you should get to while in Australia – not because everyone else goes to them, but because they are worth visiting in their own right. It is a highly personal list of top spots, in no way comprehensive. You will be able to add many more.

### SYDNEY OPERA HOUSE (BENNELONG POINT, SYDNEY, NEW SOUTH WALES)

It is difficult to explain the powerful attraction of this building, or why so many people make the pilgrimage to stand on its steps every year. It appears surprisingly small when you see it first – perhaps because you anticipate that shape made familiar by so many photos and postcards. Eventually the roof structure starts to catch the eye from all vantage points on the harbour.

As well as walking around it, preferably in sunshine when the millions of tiny tiles catch the light from different angles, venture inside. Guided tours, filled with statistics, are run every day. Try to catch a performance in one of its theatres or the concert hall instead of simply taking a tour. The scale and grandeur of the auditoria are worth experiencing. You can often get half-price tickets, those still unsold on the day of the performance, at the Half-Tix booth on Martin Place, beside the tourist information stand. Seven dollars or so to experience the National Symphony Orchestra in full flight in the concert hall is a real bargain. The atmosphere in this venue is very sophisticated, people dress up, and champagne is available to be sipped on a balcony over the harbour at the interval.

There is a waterside snack bar at the rear of the building, where you can dine and drink, in the company of lots of very greedy seagulls – watch your dinner! This spot is especially popular on Sunday mornings, when bands play. The shop in the Opera House has particularly nice, relatively cheap souvenirs, many of which are unavailable elsewhere.

## THE GREAT BARRIER REEF (QUEENSLAND)

Everyone has heard of the 2000 km-long belt of coral reefs and islands in north-eastern Queensland that makes up the Great Barrier Reef. You have to see some of its 400 varieties of coral, 10,000 species of sponge, 4000 species of molluscs and more than 1500 species of brightly coloured tropical fish. You can swim round it, scuba-dive, walk over it (watch out for the poisonous stone-fish), take a glass-bottomed boat over it or look at it through the windows of an underwater observatory. It is the world's largest marine conservation reserve (345,000 $km^2$), and most of its islands are also National Parks. The cheapest place to reach it from is probably Cairns, which offers all sorts of day trips to more accessible reefs and islands.

## KAKADU NATIONAL PARK (NORTHERN TERRITORY)

This has to be the most exciting of Australia's wonderful National Parks. It was placed on the United Nations World

Heritage List as a place to be preserved for future generations on the basis of its scenic beauty, cultural significance and ecological value. It is in a remote area, 220 km east of Darwin, but has been recently developed to be relatively easily accessible with surfaced roads, two motels and several free camp-grounds. Go there and learn about its animals, see the fantastic birds, see crocodiles undisturbed in the wild and look at some of the best examples of Aboriginal art in Australia.

## LAKE ST CLAIR–CRADLE MOUNTAIN (TASMANIA)

This is a mountainous National Park which contains a world-famous walking trail; 85 km long, it can be attempted if you are reasonably fit and adventurous, taking you through five days of some of the most beautiful scenery in the world. It is quite difficult terrain, often wet and boggy underfoot, so the Overland Track should be approached with caution. There are also numerous short bushwalks in the area, suitable for the more faint-hearted, and it is easily accessible by car and bus from either end.

Make a point of getting there, preferably to camp, and see the tame wallabies and possums that frequent the camping grounds; take a walk and enjoy the misty, mountain scenery including the highest mountain in Tasmania, Mount Ossa (1617 metres), and the deepest natural freshwater lake in Australia, Lake St Clair. If you are very lucky, you may see a platypus. There is also a lodge at the Cradle Mountain end of the Park with a nocturnal window; go there and see possums, mountain cats and the famed Tasmanian Devil fighting over the leftovers the lodge leaves out for them. This 126,205 hectare National Park is really challenging and would appeal especially to outdoor types who enjoy hard-won pleasures.

## KURANDA SCENIC RAILWAY (CAIRNS, FAR NORTH QUEENSLAND)

This little train trip, 34 km long, is a real adventure. You climb through the mountains between Cairns and the Atherton tableland, passing through 15 tunnels, deep gorges, and over sheer precipices, in a little rattling train on a twisting narrow-gauge track. High point of the journey is crossing the bridge over the spectacular Barron Falls: on one side a Niagarous waterfall, on the other a sheer drop to the gorge below.

The trip takes about two hours, and brings you to Kuranda, a pretty town where you can visit a Butterfly Sanctuary, a Nocturnal House (watch the sugar gliders making their gravity-defying leaps from tree to tree) and numerous art galleries, craft shops and other tourist attractions. There is also a market on Sunday and Wednesday mornings.

Undeniably touristy, the trip, with its views of canefields, tropical vegetation and the sea around Cairns, from an antique train and with an interesting destination, is well worth taking.


## AYERS ROCK, ALSO KNOWN AS ULURU (YULARA, NORTHERN TERRITORY)

This great red rock, the largest monolith in the world, has a definite air of mystery. Unfortunately its popularity with tourists, despite its relative remoteness, makes the path to its summit like a busy street. The walking track around its base (10 km long, an easy four hours) provides a chance to get away from the crowds and appreciate the rock's special atmosphere.

It is of tremendous spiritual significance to the Aboriginal tribes of the area, who fought for years to recover it from the tourist trade. The rather unsatisfactory solution finally reached in 1985 was the transfer of the freehold title to an Aboriginal Land Trust, who in turn lease it back to the Federal Government. Some especially important sacred sites have been fenced off and tourists are requested not to disturb them. Still, it's a poor solution in that the Aboriginals get lots of money, but not their rock back, and the tourist trade goes on.

Ayers Rock is 335 metres high above the open plain around it, 3.6 km long and 2.5 km wide. Every day hundreds of tourists climb up its sheer slopes to the summit. The view from the top is fantastic, but the ascent is quite demanding.

It's very surprising more people don't slip, or die of heart attacks, than the present statistic of a couple of deaths every year.

Made of a conglomerate of compacted gravel and boulders, and eroded into a smooth surface with many hollows by wind-driven sand, its red colour is part of its fascination. Ayers Rock would not be the same if it were grey, or brown. Part of the Great Western Plateau, like Mount Lofty above Adelaide and the Stirling and Kimberley Ranges, it is of the pre-Cambrian era, somewhere between 2600 and 600 million years old. There are neighbouring rocks of similar vintage, Mount Connor and the Olgas, which are equally fascinating. All are located in the 1325 km$^2$ of desert that make up Uluru National Park. It is 463 km from Alice Springs and can only be visited from Yulara, the resort centre specially built for the purpose.

Yulara was specially designed to blend into the scenery and replaced the jumble of hotels and campsites that had grown up around Ayers Rock's base; 450 km from Alice Springs, it is totally self-contained and can accommodate 5000 visitors with 800 resident service personnel. It has a huge campsite and two expensive hotels. There is also the Ayers Rock Lodge, the only place offering hostel-type accommodation. It gets heavily booked and is usually filled to capacity every night – if you are going to Ayers Rock, book this first. Many bus companies operate packages from Alice Springs to Yulara and Ayers Rock. These are the cheapest option, but make one feel horribly sheep-like. All leave at the same time, and visit the same points of interest. You are shepherded on and off the buses like clockwork – climb the rock at 8 a.m., tour of the base at 11.30, sunset photos at 6.30 etc., etc. Try to take an extra day – easily arranged with most companies – to explore on your own and avail yourself of the excellent ranger-guided walks at its base (far better than those of some ill-informed couriers with private bus companies). You should also see the Aboriginals' video about the rock and what it means to them – on display in Yulara Information Centre and at the rangers' station 1.5 km from its base. It is called *Uluru, an Angangu Story*.

## THE PINNACLES DESERT (NEAR CERVANTES, WESTERN AUSTRALIA)

In the Nambung National Park, 260 km north of Perth, is a strange landscape of limestone pillars. They are the product of millions of years of erosion and consist of hundreds of columns, located in a sandy desert. Some are tiny, sticking out of the sand, others are tall and strangely phallic. Their shape and sheer quantity make a marvellous sight, particularly as the light goes down and they cast long shadows. Old legends of strange petrified armies come to mind as your imagination runs riot. This little-known area is one of Australia's natural wonders, and possibly the strangest.

Cervantes is the base for seeing the Pinnacles; you can get bus trips from Perth, or go by private car. The access road is extremely rough and difficult to negotiate without a four-wheel drive vehicle.

## ★ Six Things to Avoid ★

Australia has more than its share of dangerous, and even deadly, animals. Being unused to them at home, some Poms get absolutely paranoid whenever they step outside their front doors. This is taking things too far, but it is only sensible to enquire about the dangers and to pay careful attention to advice from the locals. People who fail to do this and swim in crocodile-infested areas or shove their hands under logs where snakes may live get scant sympathy.

## STONEFISH

This member of the family *Synanceidae* is believed to be the most venomous fish in the world. Along its back are 13 spines, each of which contains two poison glands. Their venom causes intense pain and swelling and can attack the nervous system, leading, in extreme cases, to paralysis and death. They are found in estuaries and bays of eastern Australia.

143

## BOX JELLYFISH OR SEA WASP

From late November to March these jellyfish are common in the sea off northern Australia. They are transparent and nearly impossible to see in the water, with stinging tentacles stretching behind them. Any sting will cause extreme pain and scarring. A major sting may kill either directly or by causing the person to pass out and drown. During the season, do not swim in the sea except in specially netted areas. Observe the warning signs and ask local advice.

## SHARKS

Sharks of many species inhabit the waters around Australia. Most major swimming areas have nets extended out to sea, at right angles to the beach, to prevent sharks from cruising along the beach as they like to do. Pay attention to local warnings and do not swim near fish processing plants or in other places where blood and offal are discharged into the sea.

## CROCODILES

You saw the film . . . Australia has two species of crocodile: the smaller freshwater, or Johnston's Crocodile, which is harmless to man in most circumstances, and the larger, more aggressive and far more dangerous Estuarine Crocodile. Estuarine Crocodiles can be found quite far up rivers, in landlocked billabongs, and in the sea at night as they move from creek to creek. They are found from Maryborough in Queensland to the Kimberley ranges in WA. Do not camp on river banks, clean fish at the water's edge or swim in these areas unless you are certain it is safe. If you see a croc and are unsure of which species it is, keep well clear. A saltie, as Estuarine Crocodiles are also known, can outrun you over short stretches. They cannot climb trees, fortunately, but they can jump bloody high.

## SPIDERS

While all spiders have a venom for killing their prey, Australia has several species capable of killing a human. The funnel-webs – Sydney funnel-web and tree funnel-web – are found under rocks and tree roots within a 200 km radius of Sydney, and in tree trunks in NSW and Queensland respectively. Both are capable of killing a human adult. The Redback is found under stones, rubbish and houses throughout Australia and may kill an adult. There are antivenins available for the bites of these spiders, but don't bank on that. Treat all spiders with respect and use a stick if you want to poke around in fallen leaves. The black house spider's bite can also cause great pain.

## SNAKES

Australia has 110 species of snake, of which at least 28 are dangerously venomous. Some of them are among the most deadly snakes in the world. Treat any snake you see with great care and keep well away from it. In general, snakes will flee from the footfalls of an approaching human, but beware of coming on them by surprise. Observe simple common sense rules, like not running through long grass in thongs, be cautious about exploring hidden places with bare hands, and you should be all right. If you *are* unlucky, catch and kill the snake and bring it with you to hospital. For treatment purposes correct identification is vital. Alternatively, jot down a description while waiting for help.

# 11

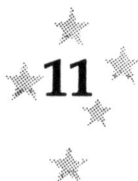

# HISTORY OF AUSTRALIA

**45 million years ago:** Australia separated from Asia and Antarctica. Animals and birds were isolated from the rest of the world and began to develop unique Australian forms, including giant kangaroos and wombats.

**2 million years ago:** Last Ice Age began, while Australia was home to huge animals and birds.

**About 40,000 years ago:** Aboriginal people began arriving in Australia from south–East Asia.

**15,000 years ago:** The huge animals began to die out. Some species, like the echidna and wombat, survived in a smaller form. Others, like the donkey-sized wombat and the 10-foot-tall kangaroo, disappeared.

**Sixth century BC:** Some evidence of contact with Australia by Chinese explorers.

**1616:** Dutchman Dirck Hartog lands at Shark Bay, Western Australia.

**1642:** Dutch sailor Abel Tasman discovers and maps south of Tasmania, naming the island Van Diemen's Land.

**1669–70:** William Dampier explores the coast of WA and decides it is not fit for human habitation.

**1770:** Captain James Cook explores the east coast of Australia and proclaims it a British possession to be called New South Wales.

**1786:** Seven years after botanist Joseph Banks recommended the establishment of a penal settlement in Australia, the British Parliament is told '. . . His Majesty has thought it advisable to fix upon Botany Bay . . .'

**1788:** First Fleet, under Captain Arthur Phillip, arrives and Phillip decides on Sydney Cove as a better site for the colony. He hoists the British flag there on 26 January. In May, the first violence between white settlers and Aborigines takes place when two Aborigines are killed at Rushcutters Bay.

**1789:** First play, *The Recruiting Officer*, put on by convicts for the King's birthday.

**1790:** Famine hits the colony and rations are cut. The Second Fleet leaves England with 1006 convicts, of whom over a quarter die on the way.

**1792:** First assisted immigration brings three farmers, a gardener, a baker, a millwright and two women with four children. The use of rum as a currency begins.

**1796:** First commercially brewed beer, first commercial theatre.

**1797:** Thirteen Merino sheep imported, and coalmining begins near the present site of Newcastle, NSW.

**1800:** The first taxes in Australia, on spirits, wine and beer, are used to build a jail.

**1802:** Matthew Flinders circumnavigates Australia in the *Investigator*. First book, *New South Wales General Standing Orders*, published in Sydney.

**1803:** First newspaper is *The Sydney Gazette and NSW Advertiser*. Van Diemen's Land settled by a small group of soldiers and convicts.

**1804:** Fifty Aborigines shot in Van Diemen's Land. Three hundred Irish convicts rebel and riot at Castle Hill, then march on Parramatta. Troops kill nine, and the six leaders are hanged.

**1806:** Captain William Bligh, having survived mutiny on the

*Bounty*, arrives as governor and tries to put down the rum trade.

**1808:** In the 'rum rebellion', the NSW Corps depose Bligh because he tries to ban the use of rum as currency, a trade which they monopolize.

**1813:** John Macarthur sells his first shipment of wool in London.

**1814:** Flinders publishes *A Voyage to Terra Australis* in which he pushes the name 'Australia' instead of 'New Holland', as the continent was then known.

**1819:** There are 26,026 people in NSW, 38% of them convicts. Van Diemen's Land has 4270 people, 47% of them convicts.

**1823:** Gold is discovered at Fish River, near Bathurst. Five-member advisory Legislative Council appointed.

**1825:** Van Diemen's Land becomes a separate colony. First settlement of Western Australia, at Albany.

**1826:** Government campaign against the Aborigines in Van Diemen's Land begins, which leads to a 3000-man effort to beat them into the natural prison of the Tasman Peninsula. This fails.

**1829:** Captain Stirling, in the *Parmelia*, brings 69 settlers from England to establish the Swan River Colony, now Perth.

**1831:** The *Sydney Herald* is established and becomes the colony's leading newspaper. It becomes the *Sydney Morning Herald* 12 years later.

**1832:** Large-scale assisted immigration begins. Over the next 37 years, 339,000 British people arrive in Australia.

**1834:** British pass an Act to set up South Australia under the rational humanistic plan drafted by Wakefield. Captain Stirling kills 80 Aborigines at the 'battle' of Pinjarra in reprisal for the death of a white man.

**1837:** Melbourne named and first overland mail service between Sydney and Melbourne established. Molesworth

Committee investigates the use of transportation of criminals. Its report, the next year, condemns transportation but does not recommend its immediate abolition.

**1839:** Governor of NSW given control of New Zealand. HMS *Beagle* discovers and names Port Darwin in honour of the scientist. When evolutionary theory becomes controversial Darwin is renamed Palmerston, only to revert to Darwin in 1911. Major W.D. Mercer imports the first pack of foxhounds. Foxes and deer are to become major pests.

**1840:** First camels imported. Transportation abolished for NSW.

**1841:** Edward John Eyre completes first crossing of the continent from east to west, despite the killing of his companion, John Baxter, by Aborigines.

**1842:** NSW's Legislative Council enlarged and Melbourne City Council established.

**1846:** First swimming championship held at the Domain Baths in Sydney.

**1848:** Ludwig Leichhardt tries to cross the continent from east to west but disappears without trace. Edmund Kennedy's expedition in Queensland ends in disaster. He is speared to death in sight of his goal and only two of the eight-man group survive.

**1850:** First convicts arrive in WA while other States agitate for an end to transportation. University of Sydney is set up.

**1851:** Gold rushes begin in the eastern States. There are 10,000 men on the NSW diggings, but when the Bendigo field opens Victoria overtakes NSW as the main gold State. NSW and Victoria separate.

**1854:** First telegraph opened. First steam train runs. Diggers rebel at Eureka Stockade under the leadership of Peter Lalor.

**1855:** Van Diemen's Land renamed Tasmania. Responsible government granted to NSW, Tasmania and Victoria. South Australia gets it in 1857, but WA does not get it until 1890.

**1856:** Victoria introduces first secret ballot in the world. NSW plays Victoria in the first inter-colony cricket match.

**1858:** Population goes above one million. Melbourne Grammar and Scotch College play the first game of what is to become Australian Rules football with 40-man teams and goals half a mile apart.

**1859:** Queensland separates from NSW and gets responsible government. Thomas Austin imports 72 partridges and 24 rabbits. By 1865, he is believed to have killed 20,000 rabbits on his property. Other Australian farmers have had to do the same ever since.

**1861:** Robert O'Hara Burke and William John Wills dies in the desert when they miss the rest of their expedition party by hours. Three thousand miners attack Chinese miners at Lambing Flat and Chinese immigration to NSW is curtailed as a result.

**1862:** Queensland starts to grow sugar commercially. John McDouall Stuart crosses the continent from south to north, providing the route for the overland telegraph that is to link Australia and Europe ten years later.

**1868:** Transportation ends when the last convict ship reaches WA. An Aboriginal cricket team tours England, the first touring Australian team. Maria Ann Smith accidentally invents the 'Granny Smith' apple.

**1873:** William Gosse discovers the biggest rock in the world, and names it after the South Australian governor, Sir Henry Ayers.

**1876:** Truganini, the last full-blooded Tasmanian Aboriginal, dies in Hobart at 73 and her body is displayed in the Tasmanian Museum for over 40 years.

**1877:** Population passes two million. First commercial telephone. First Test cricket match. Adelaide and Perth connected by telegraph.

**1879:** First successful shipment of frozen meat to Britain. Royal National Park is established, the first in Australia and the second in the world.

**1880:** First census finds 2.25 million people, not counting Aborigines. Ned Kelly, horse and cattle thief and bushranger, captured after a shoot-out at Glenrowan and is hanged in Melbourne.

**1883:** Julia Balla Guerin becomes the first woman to graduate from an Australian university. Moves towards federation of the States.

**1886:** William Guthrie Spence forms the Amalgamated Shearers' Union to fight wage-cutting by large farmers. It gains 16,000 members within a year.

**1888:** W.M. Foster starts his brewery in Victoria and the next year launches Foster's Lager on the world. Queensland and NSW get their first rail link. First successful mechanical shearing of sheep. Angus and Robertson publishing company is established.

**1891:** The first Labor Party is formed.

**1894:** Beginning of an eight-year drought which is to kill 36 million sheep. South Australia becomes first colony to give women the vote.

**1896:** Victoria introduces minimum wage. First moving pictures in Australia shown in Melbourne.

**1899:** Australia begins sending the first of 16,000 troops to the Boer War. In all, 251 men are killed and 267 die from disease during the campaign.

**1900:** On 9 July Queen Victoria gives her assent to the Commonwealth of Australia Constitution Act. Bubonic plague breaks out in Sydney. Aboriginal brothers Jimmy and Joe Governor kill seven whites, the incident that was the basis for the book *The Chant of Jimmy Blacksmith* by Thomas Keneally, published in 1972.

**1901:** Australia is federated on 1 January and the Commonwealth Public Service established. An Australian flag is selected following a competition; five almost identical entries share the prize money. It has the Union Jack, a six-pointed star below to symbolize the States, and the Southern Cross on a blue ground. Duke of York opens first national Parliament in Melbourne. Aborigines excluded from census and citizenship.

**1904:** Commonwealth Court of Conciliation and Arbitration is established to deal with industrial disputes and wage claims. WA builds an 1800-kilometre fence from Port Hedland in the north to Esperance in the south to keep rabbits out. They get through.

**1906:** What was Australia's, and is claimed to be the world's first feature film, *The Story of the Kelly Gang*, is made by Millard Johnson and William Gibson. Bondi Surf Life Saving Club is formed.

**1907:** Australia, with Canada and New Zealand, gets Dominion status. Britain consults them about foreign policy but they cannot make independent decisions. Principle of basic wage established. Rugby League begins in NSW.

**1908:** Seventh star is added to the Commonwealth flag, representing the Territories. Women in Victoria get the vote.

**1909:** Canberra chosen as site for national capital after Yass, Tumur, Bamabala, Dalgety and Albury are considered. Compulsory military training is introduced. The first legal enactment of the principle of universal liability for military service in any English-speaking country.

**1911:** Royal Australian Navy established. First Federal census finds 4,455,005 non-Aboriginal people in Australia. The transcontinental railway line, which had been used to entice WA into federation, is started.

**1912:** American architect Walter Burley Griffin designs Canberra.

**1914:** Australia enters the First World War on the side of Britain. Australian and New Zealand Army Corps (ANZAC) is set up. The first (volunteer) Australian Imperial Force of 20,000 men is raised and sails for Egypt.

**1915:** First Commonwealth income tax is introduced. Allied troops, including ANZACs, land at Gallipoli. Although Australia loses 7600 men and 19,000 are wounded in a futile campaign, this is widely seen as the coming of age of Australia. A Hawaiian, Duke Kahanamoku, demonstrates surfing on a 36-kilogram pine board.

**1916:** Returned Sailors', Soldiers' and Airmen's League (now the RSL) is founded. After Australians distinguish themselves but lose men heavily in the slaughter of the Somme, a referendum is held on the introduction of conscription and narrowly defeated.

**1917:** South Australia bans the teaching of German. The Trans-Australia Railway opens from Port Augusta to Kalgoorlie, but because of differing gauges passengers must change trains three times between Sydney and Perth. A second conscription referendum is heavily defeated.

**1918:** War ends. Of the 329,000 Australians, all volunteers, who have served overseas, 59,330 have been killed and 151,171 wounded. Australian population reaches five million. Over the next four years 35,000 British ex-servicemen and their families migrate to Australia.

**1919:** Australia is a founding member of the League of Nations. An influenza epidemic kills over 11,000. First public broadcast. Daisy May Bates, self-taught welfare worker and anthropologist, sets up the camp at Ooldea where she is to tend Aborigines until 1935.

**1920:** Queensland and Northern Territory Aerial Services (QANTAS) is formed.

**1921:** Edith Cowan becomes first woman elected to an Australian Parliament, in WA.

**1923:** Vegemite is invented by C.P. Callister.

**1924:** Sugar and koala skins exported. Voting in Federal elections becomes compulsory.

**1925:** The Prickly Pear Board, set up five years earlier, sets loose 30,000 caterpillar eggs to attack the weed and within ten years most of the plants have been exterminated.

**1926:** Western Australia begins agitating to leave the Commonwealth.

**1927:** Australasian (now Australian) Council of Trade Unions established. Federal Parliament meets for the first time in Canberra.

**1928:** Flying doctor service set up by the Rev. John Flynn. Charles Kingsford Smith and Charles Ulm make the first trans-Pacific flight in nine days.

**1929:** James Joyce's *Ulysses* banned.

**1930:** Harold Lasseter dies in the central desert searching for a spectacular reef of gold he believes exists.

**1932:** Sydney Harbour Bridge opened after a delay when F. de Groot gallops his horse to the ribbon and slashes it before the Premier can do so. He gets 2,500 letters of congratulation.

**1933:** WA votes by a large majority to leave the Commonwealth, but the British tell it that all Australia must vote to allow any State to leave. Town of Stuart renamed Alice Springs after Lady Alice Todd, wife of the Superintendent of Telegraphs for South Australia.

**1934:** Sugar growers import the cane toad to control the grey-backed beetle. The poisonous toad fails to kill the beetle and goes on to become a major pest.

**1937:** Federal and State governments agree on an enforced policy of assimilation for Aborigines into white society.

**1938:** One hundred and eighty people rescued from the sea at Bondi Beach on a single day.

**1939:** Forty-five minutes after Britain, Australia declares war on Germany. Conscription for military service at home introduced. First sliced bread.

**1941:** Australians fight in North Africa, Greece, Syria and Crete. War declared on Japan.

**1942:** Japanese make the first of 50 bombing raids on Darwin that are to kill 233 people. Over 15,000 Australians captured by Japanese after fall of Singapore. Many of them later starve or are worked to death by their captors. The battles of Coral Sea, Midway and the Kokoda Trail begin to halt the Japanese advance.

**1943:** Conscription for overseas military service. Post between Australia and Britain sent on microfilm. PAYE tax starts.

**1944:** Liberal Party formed. Japanese POWs break out of Cowra camp and 232 are killed. Meat rationed.

**1945:** War ends with 33,552 Australians killed out of a total enlistment of 926,000 men and 63,100 women.

**1946:** First celebration of Australia Day.

**1947:** Commonwealth Government buys QANTAS. Australia agrees to accept displaced Europeans and an estimated 250,000 arrive in the late 1940s and early 1950s.

**1949:** Australians became Australian citizens, but still use British passports.

**1950:** Communist Party banned. Australia enters Korean War. Myxomatosis introduced to kill rabbits. It works.

**1951:** Chiko roll invented. ANZUS defence alliance entered with New Zealand and the United States, marking a shift from dependence on Britain in defence matters.

**1952:** First British atomic bomb exploded on Monte Bello islands off coast of WA.

**1953:** Britain explodes several atomic bombs at Woomera, South Australia. Not all Aborigines are removed from the area first.

**1956:** Melbourne hosts Olympic Games. Television begins in Sydney. Edna Everage created.

**1957:** Australian Labor Party split over Communist influence. Joern Utzon designs Sydney Opera House.

**1959:** Population reaches ten million.

**1962:** First Australians sent to Vietnam. Aborigines get the right to vote in Federal elections in Queensland, WA and the Northern Territory.

**1964:** *The Australian*, published by Rupert Murdoch, becomes the first national newspaper.

**1966:** Australia gives up pounds and switches to the decimal dollar. US President Lyndon Johnson visits Australia and Prime Minister Harold Holt produces the slogan 'All the way with LBJ' as a sign of his enthusiasm. The first national servicemen are sent to Vietnam, bringing the number of Australians there to 4500.

**1967:** Ronald Ryan, hanged in Melbourne, becomes the last man executed in Australia. By a 90.8% 'yes' vote, a referendum to end all forms of legal discrimination against Aborigines is carried. They are included in the census for the first time and the Constitution is amended to allow the Federal Government as well as the States to legislate for them.

**1968:** Commonwealth Council and Office of Aboriginal Affairs founded. It becomes a Department in 1972. Australia's population reaches twelve million.

**1969:** The principle of equal pay for women is established. Standard gauge railway finally completed from Sydney to Perth.

**1970:** The Indian Pacific train service inaugurated from Perth to Sydney, one of the great train journeys of the world. It contains the longest stretch of straight track in the world, 478 kilometres. Pope Paul VI tours Australia.

**1971:** Senator Neville Bonner becomes the first Aboriginal member of an Australian Parliament. Troops begin to leave Vietnam. Jack Mundey, leader of the Builders Laborers' Federation, uses the term 'green ban' for the first time for his members' refusal to destroy landmarks and sites that they feel are significant.

**1972:** Under Gough Whitlam, the first Labor Government in 23 years is elected. The new government recognizes Communist China and withdraws the last Australian troops from Vietnam. The Gurindji Aboriginal tribe win limited legal rights to their traditional lands.

**1973:** Bob Hawke, president of the ACTU, elected unopposed as president of the Labor Party. Sydney Opera House completed after 16 years and $100 million compared with an original estimate of $7 million. Queen Elizabeth II opens it and the first production is Prokofiev's opera *War and Peace*. Patrick White wins Nobel Prize for literature with *The Eye of the Storm*.

**1974:** Woodward Report outlines the principles of Aboriginal land rights. *Advance Australia Fair* replaces *God Save the Queen* as national anthem. On Christmas Day, Cyclone Tracy destroys Darwin, killing at least 50, causing the evacuation of 30,000 and necessitating the rebuilding of most of the city.

**1975:** Law against racial discrimination comes into force. Colour television introduced. Whitlam Labor Government dismissed by the Governor-General, Sir John Kerr.

**1976:** Family Court of Australia set up and the concept of no-fault divorce, based on one year's separation, is established. Aboriginal pastor Sir Douglas Nicholls becomes governor of South Australia. *God Save the Queen* returns as national anthem.

**1977:** The country's worst rail disaster kills 80 at Granville in NSW. *The Sullivans* television series is sold to England, the first of 30 countries that buy it over the next five years.

**1978:** Northern Territory gains self-government, instead of being under South Australia. Former Prime Minister Sir Robert Menzies dies. Over the year, 47 battered vessels full of Vietnamese boat people arrive at Darwin.

**1979:** Australian diplomats ordered to leave Iran. The legal concept that Australia was an unoccupied land, without settled inhabitants or laws, at the time of the arrival of the British (which had been established in 1869) is challenged. The challenge fails.

**1980:** Bob Hawke enters Parliament. Azaria Chamberlain disappears at Ayers Rock. Her mother says she was taken by a dingo, a view accepted by the first inquest in 1981. The world's oldest fossil fish, 480 million years old, found near Alice Springs.

**1981:** Population reaches 14.9 million. There are 159,600

Aborigines. The Pitjantjatjara tribal group win land rights in South Australia. Australia's own dictionary, *The Macquarie*, is published. Rupert Murdoch buys the London *Times*.

**1982:** Unemployment reaches record levels. Controversy rages over the damming of the Franklin River in Tasmania. After a second inquest in 1981, Lindy Chamberlain is tried and found guilty of murdering her daughter and sentenced to life imprisonment.

**1983:** The 'Ash Wednesday' bushfires sweep through Victoria and South Australia, killing 68. The Labor Party is elected to power and Bob Hawke becomes Prime Minister. His new minister for Sport, Recreation and Tourism causes a storm when he describes Australia's favourite symbol, the koala, as a 'flea-ridden, piddling, stinking, scratching, rotten little thing'. Australia wins the America's Cup.

**1984:** *Advance Australia Fair* replaces *God Save the Queen* once again as national anthem. Hawke Government goes to the people and is returned with a reduced majority. Anti-nuclear protests bring 250,000 people onto the streets on Palm Sunday. Population reaches 15.45 million. The 'Bandido' and 'Commanchero' bikie gangs have a shoot-out in a pub car park in the Sydney suburb of Milperra, leaving six men and a girl of 14 dead.

**1985:** John Howard takes over from Andrew Peacock as leader of the Federal Liberal Party. Lindy Chamberlain released from prison, three years into her sentence, after widespread disquiet and public agitation about the conviction. Adelaide hosts Australia's first Formula One Grand Prix. After a long and bitter campaign, Ayers Rock is handed over to Aboriginal owners who are to lease it perpetually to the Commonwealth.

**1986:** Australia's defence of the America's Cup begins off Fremantle, Perth's port, in Western Australia. Sir Joh Bjelke-Petersen defies the polls and wins another term as Premier of Queensland. Rupert Murdoch begins a battle to take over the *Herald* and *Weekly Times* group. With his victory in 1987, the number of major newspaper owners drops from three to two. Hawke Government brings down an austere budget.

**1987:** Bob Hawke wins an historic third term as Prime Minister, despite promises early in the year not to call an early election. His victory is helped by disarray in the opposition, caused by Sir Joh's entry to Federal politics, splitting the Liberal/National Party coalition. Australia loses the America's Cup to the San Diego Yacht Club. The Federal Government struggles with the State Governments of Tasmania and Queensland over conservation. Preparations for the 1988 bicentenary get into full swing, with events planned for all parts of the country. Meryl Streep to star in *Evil Angels*, the film of the Chamberlain case. Both Chamberlains pardoned in June by the Northern Territory Attorney-General. Australia is hit hard by the world stock market crash and the man formerly reputed to be Australia's richest, Robert Holmes à Court, is said to be down to his last $50 million.

**1988:** Australia launches itself into a year-long 200th birthday party, with more pageantry, pomp, ceremony, exhibitions and re-enactments than you could shake a stick at. Millions of visitors, including the British royal family, come to the party, but the Aborigines stay away and win world-wide publicity plus some concessions from Prime Minister Bob Hawke. In December the Fitzgerald Immigration Inquiry recommends the biggest overhaul of migration policy for 20 years. A log jam of 1.25 million officially acceptable applicants worldwide creates problems. Close family members and English-speakers are to get priority. In the year to 30 June 1988 143,000 settlers arrive, 24,500 of them UK-born. In the 39th referendum since Federation, Australia's ten million voters overwhelmingly reject parliamentary reforms, which would have extended Federal power over State-run local authorities and proposed extending the maximum term of both Federal houses to four years. After 12 years in opposition, a Liberal/National Party coalition led by Nick Greiner routs the Labor Party in NSW. The Chamberlains are further vindicated when in September a Darwin Court of Appeal takes five minutes to decide there was a miscarriage of justice in their

1982 convictions for the death of their daughter Azaria. Sir William Hayden, former Labor minister, appointed by the Queen as her constitutional representative, the new Governor-General. New computerized tax system launched. It is to take ten years before the high-tech system allows automatic lodgements, instant processing and refunds from hole-in-the-wall cash machines. It is discovered that the US has lied to Australia for years about what happens at Pine Gap, the massive electronic spy station near Alice Springs.

**1989:** New Points Test to implement migration policy change announced in April. Visitor numbers to Kakadu National Park increase dramatically, to 270,000 a year. A Royal Commission reports on one of 100 Aboriginal deaths in custody since 1980. Malcolm Smith, 29, had died a day after driving a paintbrush through his eye. He had been taken from his parents at the age of 11 and since returning to his family at 19 – 'illiterate, innumerate, unskilled and with no experience of normal society' – had spent only eight months outside prison.

# 12

# USEFUL ADDRESSES
## In Britain

### ★ Official Offices ★

FEDERAL

Australian High Commission, Australia House, The Strand, London wc2b 4la. Tel. 01-379 4334 (general), 01-836 7123 (visas).

AUSTRADE (Australian Trade Commission), Australia House, The Strand, London wc2b 4la. Tel. 01-379 4334.

Australian Consulate, 80 Hanover Street, Edinburgh, eh2 2hq. Tel. 031-226 6271.

Australian Consulate, Chatsworth House, Lever Street, Manchester, m1 2dl. Tel. 061-228 1344.

STATE

Agent-General for New South Wales, 66 The Strand, London wc2n 5lz. Tel. 01-839 6651.

Agent-General for Queensland, Queensland House, 392–393 The Strand, London wc2r 0lz. Tel. 01-836 3224.

Agent-General for South Australia, South Australia House, 50 The Strand, London wc2n 5lw. Tel. 01-930 7471.

Agent-General for Victoria, Victoria House, Melbourne Place, The Strand, London wc2b 4lg. Tel. 01-836 2656.

Agent-General for Western Australia, Western Australia House, 115–116 The Strand, London WC2R OAJ. Tel. *01-240 2881*.

## ★ Travel ★

Australian Airlines, 7 Swallow Street, London W1R 8DU. Tel. *01-434 3864*.

Australian Forwarding Agency Ltd, 44 Aldwych, London WC2. Tel. *01-949 0627*.

Australian Housing and Travel, 28 Melbourne Place, London WC2. Tel. *01-836 4016*.

Australian Removal Services, 147 Masons Hill, Bromley, Kent. Tel. *01-460 8535*.

British Association of Removers Overseas, 279 Grays Inn Road, London WC1X 8SY. Tel. *01-837 3088*.

Deluxe Coach Lines, second floor, 70 Brewer Street, London W1R 3PJ. Tel. *01-434 0725*.

Garuda Indonesian Airways, 35 Duke Street, London W1M 5DF. Tel. *01-486 3011*.

Malaysian Airline Systems (MAS), 25–27 St George's Street, Hanover Square, London W1R 9RE. Tel. *01-499 6286*.

Qantas Ltd, Qantas House, 395 King Street, Hammersmith, London W6 9NJ. Tel. *01-748 3131* or *0345 747767* (toll free) for reservations. (Offices also in Bristol, Birmingham, Manchester, Glasgow and Leeds.)

Railways of Australia, c/o Compass, 46 Albemarle Street, London W1X 4EP. Tel. *01-408 4141*.

REHO Travel, 13–17 New Oxford Street, London WC1A 1BH. Tel. *01-242 5555*.

Singapore Airlines, 143–147 Regent Street, London W1. Tel. *01-747 0007*.

Trailfinders, 42–48 Earls Court Road, London W8 6EJ. Tel. *01-938 3366*.

Australian Union of Students Student Travel Ltd, 117 Euston Road, London NW1. Tel. *01-388 2261*.

Youth Hostels Association, 14 Southampton Street, London WC2. Tel. *01-836 8541*.

## ★ Australian Banks ★

Commonwealth Bank, third floor, 1 Kingsway, London WC2B 6DU. Tel. *01-379 0955*.

Westpac Bank, Walbrook House, 23 Walbrook, London EC4N 8LD. Tel. *01-626 4500*.

State Bank of Victoria, Melbourne House, 48 Aldwych, London WC2B 4RA. Tel. *01-379 7966*.

Australian and New Zealand Bank (ANZ), 13 St James's Square, London SW1Y 4LF. Tel. *01-930 1461*.

State Bank of South Australia, 29 Pall Mall, London SW1Y 5LR. Tel. *01-489 0300*.

Rural and Industries Bank of Western Australia, (R&I), Park House, 16 Finsbury Circus, London EC2M 7DJ. Tel. *01-256 5600*.

## ★ Tourist Offices ★

Australian Tourist Commission (ATC), fourth floor, 20 Savile Row, London W1X 1AE. Tel. *01-434 4371*. (Also Tourism Tasmania, Northern Territory and Western Australia Tourism Commissions.)

Canberra Tourist Bureau, c/o Australian Destination Centre, 27 High Street, Windsor, Berks, SL4 1LH. Tel. *0753-855 457*.

New South Wales Tourist Commission, 66 The Strand, London WC2N 5LZ. Tel. *01-839 6651*.

Queensland Tourist and Travel Corporation, Queensland House, 392 The Strand, London WC2R 0LZ. Tel. *01-836 1333*.

South Australian Department of Tourism, South Australia House, 50 The Strand, London WC2N 5LW. Tel. *01-930 7471*.

Victorian Tourism Commission, Victoria House, Melbourne Place, The Strand, London WC2B 4LA. Tel. *01-836 2656*.

## ★ General ★

Australian British Chamber of Commerce, Suite 615 Linen Hall, 162-168 Regent Street, London W1R 5TB. Tel. *01-439 0086*.

Australian Broadcasting Corporation (ABC), 54 Portland Place, London W1. Tel. *01-631 4456*.

Australian Reunion and Holiday Club, 200 Buckingham Palace Road, London SW1. Tel. *01-821 4108*.

Australian Studies Centre, 27 Russell Square, London WC1. Tel. *01-580 5876*.

Britain-Australia Society, Cleveland House, 19 St James's Square, London SW1Y 4JG. Tel. *01-930 5123*.

Commonwealth Institute, Kensington High Street, London W8. Tel. *01-603 4535*.

Flinders Australian Bookshop, 45 Burton Street, London WC1. Tel. *01-388 6080*.

## ★ Australian Publications ★

*Australian Outlook*, 32 Station Road, Town Hall Square, Bexhill-on-Sea, East Sussex, TN40 1RG. Tel. *0424-223 111*.

*TNT Magazine*, 52 Earls Court Road, London W8 6EJ. Tel. *01-937 3985*.

*New Australasian Express* and *LAM*, 15 Abingdon Road, London W8 6AF. Tel. *01-938 4911* (LAM Tel. *01-938 1811*).

# In Australia

## ★ Accommodation ★

### ADELAIDE

HOSTELS

AYHA Hostel, 290 Gilles Street, Adelaide 5000. Tel. *223 6007*.

Backpackers Hostel, 263 Gilles Street, Adelaide 5000. Tel. *223 5680*. (Both under $10 for a dorm bed.)

YMCA Hostel, 76 Flinders Street, Adelaide 5000. Tel. *223 1611*. (Takes guests of either sex, central and comfortable with a cheap cafeteria. Dorms, singles and doubles, with weekly rates.)

HOTELS

Afton Private Hotel, 260 South Terrace, Adelaide 5000. Tel. *223 3416*.

Metropolitan Hotel, 46 Grote Street, Adelaide 5000. Tel. *515 471*. (Both central and relatively inexpensive, with a room for about $25.)

### BRISBANE

HOSTELS

AYHA Hostel, 390 Upper Roma Street, Brisbane 4000. Tel. *221 0961*. (Also 8 km out of town at 15 Mitchell Street, Kedron, tel. *571 245*. About $6 a night.)

HOTELS

Budget Yale Inn, 413 Upper Edward Street, Brisbane 4000. Tel. *832 1663*. (With breakfast, singles around $24, doubles around $34.)

Dorchester Holiday Flats, 484 Upper Edward Street, Brisbane 4000. Tel. *831 2967*.

Tourist Motel, 555 Gregory Terrace, Brisbane 4000. Tel. *524 171*. (Central, with cooking facilities. Room only ranges from $17 to $25 for one person, $16 to $20 each for two.)

Ruth Fairfax House (CWA Private Hotel), 89 Gregory Terrace, Brisbane 4000. Tel. *831 8188*.


## DARWIN

### HOSTELS

AYHA Hostel, Beaton Road, Berrimah 5789. Tel. *843 902*. (Unfortunately 12 km from the city centre, otherwise good, with bike hire and cheap trips organized from the hostel.)

YMCA Hostel, Doctor's Gully, Darwin 5790. Tel. *818 377*.

YWCA Hostel, 119 Mitchell Street, Darwin 5790. Tel. *818 644*. (With similar central locations, both Ys take men and women and offers a range of dorms and rooms, with good weekly rates. The YWCA may be slightly cheaper at around $20 single, $25 double. Both get full, so book ahead.)


### HOTELS

Lameroo Lodge, 69 Mitchell Street, Darwin 5790. Tel. *819 733*. (Wide range of dorms, rooms and rooms with facilities.)

Larrekeyah Lodge, 50 Mitchell Street, Darwin 5790. Tel. *817 550*.


## MELBOURNE

### HOSTELS

AYHA Hostel, 500 Abbotsford Street, North Melbourne 3051. Tel. *328 2880*. Also 76 Chapman Street, North Melbourne 3051. Tel. *328 3595*. (Close together, some 3 km from the city centre. About $11 for a dorm.)

YWCA Family Hostel, 489 Elizabeth Street, Melbourne 3000. Tel. *329 5188*. (Right in town, on the main street and near terminals for airport and inter-city buses. It is expensive, about $40 for a double, but that includes en suite bathroom in a luxurious modern room.)

## HOTELS

Victoria Hotel, 215 Little Collins Street, Melbourne 3000. Tel. *630 441*. (Budget rooms at about $33 for one person, $40 for two.)

Spencer Motel, 44 Spencer Street, Melbourne 3000. Tel. *626 991*. (Singles from $19 to $44, doubles $56.)

Domain, 52 Darling Street, South Yarra 3141. Tel. *266 3701*.


## PERTH

### HOSTELS

AYHA Hostel, 62 Newcastle Street, Perth 6000. Tel. *328 1135*. Also 46 Francis Street. Tel. *328 7794*. (Both offer dorm beds for under $10.)

YMCA, Jewell House, 180 Goderich Street, Perth 6000. Tel. *325 1085*. (Caters for long-term stays, with kitchen facilities. Singles are about $22, doubles $32.)

YMCA Hostel, 119 Murray Street, Perth 6000. Tel. *325 2744*.

Travel Mates Hostel, 496 Newcastle Street, Perth 6000. Tel. *328 6685*.

Top Notch Hostel, 194 Aberdeen Street, Perth 6000. Tel. *328 6667*. (Both offer facilities – and prices – similar to AYHA hostels.)


### HOTELS

CWA House (CWA Private Hotel), 1174 Hay Street, West Perth 6005. Tel. *321 6081*. (Bed and breakfast around $25 single, $48 double.)

City Waters Lodge, 118 Terrace Road, Perth 6000. Tel. *325 5020*. (Self-contained units around $45; central and near the lovely Swan River).

Angelo Lodge, 66 Riversdale Road, Rivervale 6103. Tel. *361 7944*. (Self-contained apartments 4 km from the city centre. Around $40 for two people.)

## SYDNEY

### HOSTELS

AYHA Hostel, 28 Ross Street, Parramatta Road, Forest Lodge. Tel. *692 0747*. Also 407 Marrickville Road, Dulwich Hill. Tel. *569 0272*. (Both are rather far from the centre and cost about $11 a night in a dormitory. Similar rates can be found in the more convenient Kings Cross area.)

YWCA Hostel, 5–11 Wentworth Avenue, Sydney 2010. Tel. *264 2451*. (At the corner of Liverpool Street – very central – this has a good cheap cafeteria and lower rates for longer stays. Women and couples around $15 for a bed in a small dorm, twice that for single rooms.)

Kings Cross Backpackers Hostel, 162 Victoria Street, Kings Cross 2011. Tel. *356 3232*. (Good for making work/travelling contacts, buying cars etc. Double rooms $10 per person, dorms $9.)

Young Cross Country Travellers Centre (The Downunder Hostel), 25 Hughes Street, Kings Cross 2011. Tel. *358 1143*. (Basic, but also has good notice board.)

Young Travellers Hostel, 15 Roslyn Gardens, Kings Cross 2011. Tel. *357 3509*. (Dorms only, $8 a night.)

### HOTELS

Springfield Lodge, 9 Springfield Avenue, Kings Cross 2011. Tel. *358 3222*. ($24 single, $28 double, with discounts for week-long stays. Rooms have light cooking facilities – fridge, toaster, kettle – which makes eating a lot cheaper.)

Sydney Tourist Hotel (Pacific Coast Budget Accommodation), 400 Pitt Street, Sydney 2000. Tel. *211 5777*.

CB Private Hotel, 417 Pitt Street, Sydney 2000. Tel. *211 5115*. (Both the above two offer basic, low-budget accommodation in the city centre. Single rooms $22/$17, doubles $32/$26). George Hotel, 700a George Street, Sydney 2000. Tel. *211 1800*. (Single, doubles and dorms, discounts for overseas students.)

## AUSTRALIAN YOUTH HOSTELS ASSOCIATION (AYHA) STATE OFFICES

AYHA hostels vary in quality and the range of services they provide. To generalize, those in major population centres are often overcrowded and do not match private hostels for comfort or atmosphere. Outside the cities there are some gems – small, friendly and often in attractive old buildings. All provide cooking facilities. Their notice boards are a useful source of cheap travel opportunities and informal information exchange. Charges range between $6 and $12 for dorms – some also provide single, double and family rooms. Sleeping sheets are compulsory. It is sometimes necessary to book at the State office before going to the hostel itself.

New South Wales: 60 Mary Street, Surry Hills, Sydney 2010. Tel. *212 1151*.

Northern Territory: Darwin Hostel, Beaton Road, Berrimah 5789. Tel. *843 902*.

Queensland: 462 Queen Street, Brisbane 4000. Tel. *831 2022*.

South Australia: 1 Sturt Street, Adelaide 5000. Tel. *515 583*.

Tasmania: 28 Criterion Street, Hobart 7000. Tel. *349 617*.

Victoria: 205 King Street, Melbourne 3000. Tel. *670 7991*.

Western Australia: 257 Adelaide Terrace, Perth 6000. Tel. *325 5844*.

## ★  British Representatives  ★

British High Commission, Commonwealth Avenue, Yarralumla, Canberra, ACT 2600.

British Consul-General, Goldfields House, 1 Alfred Street, Sydney Cove, Sydney, NSW 2000.

British Consul-General, CML Building, 330 Collins Street, Melbourne, VIC 3000.

Honorary Consul-General, Hassell Pty Ltd, 70 Hindmarsh Square, Adelaide, SA 5000.

British Consul-General, BP House, 193 North Quay, Brisbane, QLD 4000.

British Consul-General, Prudential Building, 95 St George's Terrace, Perth, WA 6000.

British Council, Edgecliff Centre, 203–233 New South Head Road, PO Box 88, Edgecliff, NSW 2027.

## ★ Major Commonwealth Employment Service (CES) Offices ★

Adelaide: 45 Grenfell Street, Adelaide, SA 5000.
        321 King William Street, Adelaide SA 5000.

Brisbane: Block B, 232 Adelaide Street, Brisbane, QLD 4000.

Darwin: Palmeston Building, corner Cavenach and Knuckey Streets, Darwin, NT 5790.

Melbourne: 367 Collins Street, Melbourne, VIC 3000.

Perth: 256 Adelaide Terrace, Perth, WA 6000. 44 St George's Terrace, Perth, WA 6000.

Sydney: 818 George Street, Railway Square, Broadway, Sydney, NSW 2000.

## ★ Customs ★

Enquiries should be addressed to the Collector of Customs at the port where the goods are to be imported.

The Collector of Customs Sydney, NSW 2000. Tel. *02-226 5000*. Telex: *73909*.

The Collector of Customs Melbourne, Victoria 3000. Tel. *03-611 1555*. Telex: *30956*.

The Collector of Customs Brisbane, Queensland 4000. Tel. *07-835 0444*. Telex: *40183*.

The Collector of Customs Port Adelaide, South Australia 5015. Tel. *08-479 211*. Telex: *82155*.

The Collector of Customs Fremantle, Western Australia 6160. Tel. *09-430 1444*. Telex: *92744*.

The Collector of Customs Hobart, Tasmania 7000. Tel. *002-301 201*. Telex: *58009*.

The Collector of Customs Darwin, Northern Territory 5790. Tel. *089-814 444*. Telex: *85043*.

The Comptroller-General, Australian Customs Service, Canberra, ACT 2600. Tel. *062-723 922*. Telex: *62049*.

Business Customs Enquiries: Department of Industry and Commerce, Barton, Canberra, ACT 2600.

Quarantine Enquiries: The Australian Quarantine Service, Department of Health, PO Box 100, Woden, ACT 2606.

## ★ Motoring Organizations ★

Australian Capital Territory: National Roads and Motorists' Association (NRMA), 92–96 Northbourne Avenue, Canberra, ACT 2601. Tel. *438 888*.

New South Wales: National Roads and Motorists' Association (NRMA), 151 Clarence Street, Sydney, NSW 2000. Tel. *260 9222*.

Northern Territory: Automobile Association of the Northern Territory (AANT). 79–81 Smith Street, Darwin, NT 5790. Tel. *813 837*.

Queensland: Royal Automobile Club of Queensland (RACQ), 300 St Paul's Terrace, Fortitude ʹalley, Brisbane, QLD 4006. Tel. *253 2444*.

South Australia: Royal Automobile Association of South Australia (RAA), 41 Hindmarsh Square, Adelaide, SA 5000. Tel. *223 4555*.

Tasmania: Royal Automobile Club of Tasmania (RACT), corner Murray and Patrick Streets, Hobart, TAS 7000. Tel. *382 200*.

Victoria: Royal Automobile Club of Victoria (RACV), 123 Queen Street, Melbourne. VIC 3000. Tel. *607 2211*.

Western Australia: Royal Automobile Club of Western Australia (RACWA). 228 Adelaide Terrace, Perth, WA 6000. Tel. *421 4444*.

# ★ National Trust ★

Australian Capital Territory: 42 Franklin Street, Manuka 2603, ACT.

New South Wales: Observatory Hill, Sydney 2000, NSW.

Northern Territory: 14 Knuckey Street, Darwin 5790 (GPO Box 3520) NT.

Queensland: Old Government House, George Street, Brisbane 4000, (GPO Box 1494), QLD.

South Australia: Ayers House, 288 North Terrace, Adelaide 5000, SA.

Tasmania: 25 Kirkway Place, Hobart 7000, TAS.

Victoria: Tasma Terrace, Parliament Place, Melbourne 3002, VIC.

Western Australia: Old Perth Boys School, 139 St George's Terrace, Perth 6000, WA.

# ★ National Park Organizations ★

Australian Capital Territory: National Parks and Wildlife Service, third floor, Construction House, 217 Northbourne Avenue, Turner 2601.

New South Wales: National Parks and Wildlife Service, 189–193 Kent Street, Sydney 2000.

Northern Territory: National Parks and Wildlife Service, first floor, Commercial Union Building, Smith Street, Darwin 5794.

Queensland: National Parks and Wildlife Service, 239 George Street, Brisbane 4000.

South Australia: National Parks and Wildlife Service, 129 Green-hill Road, Unley 5061.

Tasmania: National Parks and Wildlife Service, 16 Magnet Court, Sandy Bay 7005.

Victoria: National Parks Service, 240 Victoria Parade, East Melbourne 3002.

Western Australia: National Parks Authority, Hackett Drive, Crawley 6009.

## ★ Settlement Agencies and Associations ★

United Kingdom Settlers Association, PO Box 221, Fitzroy, Melbourne, VIC 3065. Tel. *419 3788*.

The Australia–Britain Society, twelfth floor, 55 Elizabeth Street, Sydney, NSW 2000. Tel. *231 2341*.

Australian Institute of Multicultural Affairs, GPO Box 2470V, Melbourne, VIC 3001. Tel. *608 1777*.

Federation of Ethnic Communities' Councils of Australia, fifth floor, 541 George Street, Sydney, NSW 2000. Tel. *267 9722*.

Department of Immigration, Local Government and Ethnic Affairs, Central Office, Benjamin Offices, Chan Street, Belconnen, ACT 2617. Tel. *641 111*.

## ★ Tourist Offices ★

*Australian Capital Territory Government Tourist Bureau*

City offices: Canberra, Melbourne, Sydney. Head office: ACT Government Tourist Bureau, Jolimont Centre, Northbourne Avenue, Canberra 2601. Tel. *062-49 7555*.

*West Australian Government Travel Centres (Holiday WA)*

City offices: Perth, Melbourne, Sydney, Brisbane, Adelaide. Head office: Holiday WA, 772 Hay Street, Perth 6000. Tel. *09-322 2999*.

*Victorian Government Travel Centres*

City offices: Melbourne, Sydney, Canberra, Brisbane, Adelaide, Perth, Hobart. Head office: Victorian Government Travel Centre, 230 Collins Street, Melbourne 3000. Tel. *03-602 9444*.

*Tasmanian Government Tourist Bureau (Tasbureau)*

City offices: Hobart, Melbourne, Sydney, Brisbane, Adelaide, Perth, Canberra. Head office: Tasbureau, 80 Elizabeth Street, Hobart 7000. Tel. *002-34 6911*.

*Queensland Government Travel Centres*

City offices: Brisbane, Sydney, Canberra, Melbourne, Adelaide, Perth. Head office: Queensland Government Travel Centre, corner Adelaide and Edward Streets, Brisbane 4000. Tel. *07–31 2211.*

*South Australian Government Travel Centres*

City offices: Adelaide, Melbourne, Sydney. Head office: South Australian Government Travel Centre, 18 King William Street, Adelaide 5000. Tel. *08-212 1644.*

*Travel Centres of New South Wales*

City offices: Sydney, Brisbane, Melbourne, Adelaide. Head office: NSW Government Travel Centre, 16 Spring Street (corner Pitt and Spring), Sydney 2000. Tel. *02-231 4444.*

*Northern Territory Government Tourist Bureau*

City offices: Darwin, Melbourne, Sydney, Perth, Hobart, Brisbane, Adelaide, Canberra. Head office: Northern Territory Government Tourist Bureau, 27 Smith Street, Darwin 5750. Tel. *089-81 6611.*

# 13

# BOOKS ABOUT AUSTRALIA

*Australia Travellers Guide*, Australian Tourist Commission. The (free) tourist information book available from the ATC. 112 pages of useful information, glossy photos and little maps of every city and state.

*Australia in Brief 1988*, Australian Government Publishing Service, Canberra 1988. 37th edition of the series, 80pp. This (free) booklet has replaced the *Australia Handbook* as the Department of Foreign Affairs and Trade's official handout. It is shorter and smaller – pocket-sized – and expensively produced, with a rather uninspired selection of colour photographs. It is a good general introduction to the Australian economy, but contains less specific information than its predecessor. An overview rather than a detailed rundown on the facts and figures for each area.

*Living in Australia – A Guide for New Settlers*. Australian Government Publishing Service, Canberra 1988. 191pp. People who are approved for migration get this free. A useful, if simple, outline of the way society is organized and who does what. The first 18 pages set the tone – basic advice on every kind of emergency that could blight the migrant's life in the Lucky Country. This is an extract from p.9 – under the 'Dentist' heading: 'If a tooth is knocked out: 1) find it; 2) suck it clean (do not wash in water – saliva is important); 3) put it back in position; 4) hold it there firmly; 5) go to a dentist.

Your best chance of getting the tooth to take root again is to put it back within 30 minutes.'

*The Australian Almanac*, Angus and Robertson, London and Sydney 1985. 800pp. This paperback, printed on cheap paper, places its emphasis on what is available rather than what is useful. It serves as a background reference book on many areas of Australian life as well as including a great deal of international information.

*The Concise Australian Reference Book*, Golden Press, Sydney 1986. 504pp. This neat hardback is packed with useful information about Australia, including much that you will never need unless you are world champion class in Trivial Pursuit. It is well organized and the information is grouped into logical areas of interest.

*Long Stays in Australia*, by Maggie Driver, David and Charles, Newton Abbot 1987. 190pp. This hardback book is written in a chatty style but is rather short on facts. One in a series of 'long stays' guides, it tries to introduce the Australian lifestyle to English people who are considering settling in Australia.

*A Practical Guide to Obtaining Permanent Residence in Australia*, by Adrian Joel, Legal Books, Sydney 1988. 110pp. Written by a lawyer who also gives seminars on Australian immigration policy, this is a synopsis of official literature from the Department of Immigration (DILGEA). It deals in detail with the categories of, and processes for, migration applications. Policy has changed considerably; this edition needs updating.

*Australia – A Travel Survival Kit*, by Tony Wheeler, Lonely Planet, Melbourne 1986. 616 pp. An excellent buy for those touring Australia. Lonely Planet, the guide-book publishers for the budget traveller, started out in Australia – and they know it best. This bulky paperback crams in at least a few lines for just about everywhere, plus travel and accommodation information. Work, visas and the social system are beyond its scope, but it is a must for the holidays. A new update is eagerly awaited – treat the prices with caution.

*The Insider's Guide to Australia*, by Robert Wilson, Merehurst Press, London 1987. 220pp. This paperback guide is a typical tourist's city-by-city rundown, illustrated with photographs and maps. It has plenty on where to go, how to travel and what to see. Although good, it cannot beat Lonely Planet for truly 'insider' information.

*Frommer's Australia On $30 A Day*, by John Godwin, Simon and Schuster, New York 1988. 261pp. A fairly standard tourist guide, but with excellent short-term accommodation listings for each major tourist destination, and a plethora of restaurant suggestions for those who intend to eat their way round the Lucky Country.

*Work Your Way Around the World*, by Susan Griffith, Vacation Work, Oxford 1987. Though Australia takes up only 22 of its 383 pages this book provides an introduction to the range of casual work that is available to the working holidaymaker. Other useful titles from the Vacation Work press include *The Directory of Summer Jobs Abroad, The Directory of Jobs and Careers Abroad* and *Adventure Holidays*.


And on a lighter note: *G'day! Teach Yourself Australian*, Colin Bowles, Angus & Robertson, London and Sydney, 1986. 20 easy language lessons – the only guide you'll ever need to speaking 'strine'! *No Worries; How to Survive Australians*, Robert Treborlang, Angus & Robertson, London and Sydney, 1988. A handbook of Antipodean oneupmanship that tells you how to cope with the Australian mentality! *The World's Best Aussie Jokes*, A. N. Ocker, Angus & Robertson, London and Sydney, 1986. Jokes and cartoons for every occasion.